Best wishes

[illegible]

Mary Hayden has always enjoyed adding value and making a difference in an individual's business. She loves to remove the pain and replace it with more streamlined systems. Her passion for teaching these skills has enabled many to simply and quickly realise their potential. As a Business and Operations specialist, she has a lifetime of national and international experience in finance, project and people management, and she will help you set your business up for seamless growth and success.

Dee Hutchinson, Founder, Dee is for Digital

I was immediately impressed by Mary's business knowledge, enthusiasm, practical solutions, and passion for helping business owners. She has unique skills combining her finance qualification with a process-driven approach underpinned by her LEAN Six-Sigma Qualification. This approach allows her to look at a business end to end and figure out efficient and effective solutions that contribute significantly to the bottom line.

Tony Dignam, CEO, The Agile Executive

Mary Hayden has been a really critical part of our growth at Veri Connect since we met her about two years ago. She has been a wonderful part-time CFO and a rock of sense who can integrate accountancy/ financial reporting/ booking keeping with the other business pillars. This growth is due to her work ethic and interest in getting down to the basic building blocks - I couldn't recommend her book more.

Ann-Marie McSorley, Founder and CEO, Veri Connect

Mary has a lot more than accounting to offer. She solves problems before they become problems.

Rachel Doyle, Founder, Arboretum Garden Ltd

This edition printed and bound in the Republic of Ireland by

Lettertec Ireland

Springhill House,

Carrigtwohill

Co. Cork

Republic of Ireland

www.lettertecbooks.com

The views expressed are based on the author's experience and study. They should not be taken as professional advice. The reader is responsible for his or her own actions.

From the Ground

THE 10 BASIC
BUILDING BLOCKS
FOR BUSINESS

Mary Hayden

Business and Operations Specialist

Cover image & design: Catriona Maher – Cida Designs, Carlow, Ireland

Illustrations: Nikolai Viljoen – Outside Box, South Africa

Disclaimer: The views expressed are based on the author's experience and study. They should not be taken as professional advice. The reader is responsible for his or her own actions.

CONTENTS

FOREWORD

In order to generate the financial resources necessary to provide the public services and public infrastructure that we all rely on in our everyday lives, it is essential to create and sustain a properly functioning economy. Economic growth generates tax revenues, and those financial resources are, in turn, used to help create a functioning society.

Businesses and entrepreneurs are the most important ingredient of a functioning economy as they generate employment and economic value; ultimately, they are the key drivers of economic activity. The bottom line is that business is a very significant contributor to a functioning economy and a functioning society, and as such, it should be cherished and supported to the greatest extent possible. Very often, they are not, and this needs to change.

Ireland has a large number and a wide variety of different types of businesses, but the majority are classified as SMEs (Small and Medium Enterprises), employing less than 250 people. In 2020, the country boasted 278,862 active enterprises in the business economy, with 1.63 million people engaged in those enterprises. Of those enterprises, 99.8 per cent or 278,196, were classified as SMEs and accounted for 65.6 per cent of the total persons engaged, equivalent to 1.07 million persons. Just 666 large enterprises were employing more than 250 persons, but they accounted for 34.4 per cent of the total engaged in business activities, or 560,832 persons. These businesses are dispersed all over the countryside and are an essential ingredient for more balanced regional economic growth and development. Without those businesses, we would not have a functioning economy or a functioning society.

It is difficult to speak about a generic business, as the Irish economy is populated by thousands of businesses of varying sizes that are engaged in a wide variety of different business activities across the services sector and industry. However, the one thing they all have in common is the entrepreneurial endeavour and hard work needed to make a business survive and be successful. The nature of challenges faced are common to all businesses to varying degrees.

An appropriate definition of an entrepreneur is *a person who sets up a business or businesses, taking on financial risks in the hope of profit.*' Creating and sustaining a successful business is very difficult, and the life of an entrepreneur is immensely challenging, but for many, it is also immensely rewarding.

Between 2010 and 2019, the CSO (Central Statistics Office) estimates that there were 84,195 enterprise births and 82,931 enterprise deaths in Ireland. Businesses fail for many different reasons. The reasons for failure generally include factors such as a deterioration in the economic environment; intense competition from domestic or external sources; increased costs and a squeezing of margins; the loss of a major client; or simply due to a lack of varied skills needed to run and grow a successful business.

Trading conditions for many businesses have been extremely challenging in recent years. The advent of a global pandemic in March 2020 and the subsequent imposition of significant restrictions on many business and consumer activities created enormous difficulties. While there was an unprecedented level of financial and other support from the Government, the legacy of the pandemic was very real coming into 2022.

Then, the Russian invasion of Ukraine happened, and an already challenging business environment was made even more challenging.

The war has had a very negative impact on already stretched supply chains; the various costs of doing business have increased significantly across the board; inflation has accelerated to the highest levels seen in more than three decades; interest rates are on the way up again, albeit from artificially low levels; the recruitment and retention of appropriately skilled labour is a major challenge; exchange rate markets have become quite volatile, with dollar strength and sterling weakness key themes of relevance to some Irish businesses; and the global economic outlook is now deeply uncertain as we move towards 2023.

While the domestic Irish economy remained largely immune to the very challenging external developments for much of 2022, some signs of weakness are now emerging. It seems inevitable that the domestic economic environment will become more challenging in 2023, but this, too shall pass.

In the world of business and economics, the safest mantra is always to expect and be as prepared as possible for the unexpected. Economic and business cycles have always been with us, and there are always shocks lurking in the undergrowth. That, unfortunately, is the nature of running an economy or a business. Careful control of costs and protecting the balance sheet is always advisable during economically challenging times, and those businesses with strong balance sheets can very often grasp the opportunity in the face of adversity. For others, it is simply a question of survival.

The reality for any business, but smaller businesses, in particular, is that they are very often good at doing what they do, as in producing a specific good or service. However, they may lack the requisite skills in areas such as financial management; product innovation; business planning; strategy formulation; legal issues; prioritisation of issues; marketing; productivity management; business agility; and human resource management. In short, many business owners lack the necessary skills and resources needed to bring the business to the next level and add real value. If this is the reality, those business owners should seek as much external assistance as possible, such as advice or mentoring.

Occasionally somebody will come along and offer invaluable advice in these areas and others. This book is exactly what this publication, '***From the Ground Up – 10 Basic Building Blocks For Business,*** ' attempts to do. The business-savvy author Mary Hayden addresses many of these areas and others in a very understandable, practical and straightforward manner. The progression through the book is done in a very logical way. It moves seamlessly through Business Foundations, Systems, Customers, Employees, Cashflow, Accounting, Budgets, Dashboards, and Taxation and culminates in a valuable guide to Business Supports. This is a pretty comprehensive list of essential business issues.

These are all areas that business owners need to understand to achieve success. The author outlines what business owners are trying to accomplish under many different headings, which can become overwhelming for many business owners. Hence, a publication such as this could be the difference between success and failure.

Government can do much to create the environment and provide some of the support that businesses need to survive, but much more is required. This book does precisely this by arming business leaders and owners with invaluable help and information to run a business successfully.

Jim Power - Independent Economist

DEDICATION

I dedicate this book to my father,
who always knew what question to ask.

INTRODUCTION

I have dedicated this book to my father, Jimmy Kavanagh. The man who challenged me with some great questions from a very young age. The question that sticks with me the most is, "Why not you?". His standard response whenever I questioned my abilities, and it still echoes in my head today.

The importance and power of asking great questions have been a recurring theme throughout my career and is the main reason I wanted to write a book, to enable business owners to ask themselves and their employees some great questions.

In my experience, most business owners already know enough to run and grow great businesses, but they may not always ask themselves the right questions.

By reading this book, I hope you'll be encouraged to ask yourself some tough questions to help take your business to the next level. I also hope that you'll find answers to questions you didn't even know to ask.

So let's get started!

THE FACTS

Fact #1 - One in three businesses fails in its first five years.

This fact is a shocking statistic, but it's important to remember that a large part of these failures is due to a lack of basic knowledge about running a successful business, specifically regarding topics like financial management, cash flow and funding eligibility. Most business owners I work with have excellent products and services; they are hard-working and motivated to succeed, but unfortunately, that often isn't enough.

We often hear "the devil is in the detail"; however, I believe "the devil is in the boring basics". No matter how unique your product is, if you don't understand your business's financial and commercial aspects, you increase your likelihood of failure or, at the very least, delay your success.

I don't want you to be another statistic, and I think it's safe to assume you don't want that for yourself too!

On the bright side, everything you need to know has been laid out clearly and succinctly for you in this book. You no longer have to worry about what you don't know and start to increase your confidence as a well-rounded, commercially savvy entrepreneur.

Fact #2 - Many business owners underestimate the importance of financial and commercial knowledge.

As a business owner myself, I understand that we can easily get caught up in the day-to-day running of our business and lose sight of the bigger picture. Don't make this mistake.

It is essential to focus on the operational aspects of your business, but if you have a good understanding of the financial and commercial side of things, you will be successful in the long term.

This element is an area that many business owners struggle with, and I think it's because they simply don't know where to start. This book covers all the basics you need to know to run a successful business.

So if you're feeling overwhelmed or like you're "in over your head", don't worry; use this book as a guide to rely on whenever you need it.

Fact #3 - We are in for some tough times ahead

As mentioned in Jim Power's foreword for this book, we are on the cusp of a potential worldwide recession.

At the time of writing this book, there is still a war raging in Ukraine, and the cost of operating businesses is unlike any experience before. So the need for solid, resilient and agile business foundations is more critical than ever.

Business owners must prioritise reviewing how efficiently they are operating their companies and whether they can withstand the storm to come.

The guidance in this book will provide some direction on where to look inside your business for opportunities to improve, save and grow efficiently, no matter the external environment.

THIS BOOK IS FOR YOU

This book is for you if you want to take your business to the next level. It dives into essential topics such as finance, people, cash flow, systems, taxation and information management—all of which are crucial for any thriving business.

No matter how much experience you have as a business owner, there is always room to learn more, right?

This book provides straightforward explanations and practical advice you can apply to your business immediately. Whether you're just starting in business or you've been in business for years, it will give you the foundation to build a solid and successful business that can withstand even the toughest of challenges.

It helps you to focus your current resources on increasing the bottom line through capacity and capability planning while keeping you aligned with your strategic goals. It will give you your time back to focus "on" your business rather than "in" your business. It will help you make better decisions and understand their consequences. It helps you better understand the individual sections of your business and how they affect your business as a whole. You must ensure that all departments are interconnected and that communication is open and smooth. Because too often, we pay attention to a particular part of the business to the detriment of others.

That is why I decided to use the metaphor of Building Blocks. If you were to build a house, you start "from the ground" with solid foundations, each building block being equally crucial as the next. If you don't know much about a particular block/area, it doesn't mean leaving it out; you can outsource or hire in the skill to ensure you get it right. Similarly, with your business, you can do the same.

And most importantly, this book is for you if you consider yourself to be "right-brained" and numbers make your head spin. I promise it won't be as dry or dull as you think. The goal is to empower you with questions and give you a strong foundation so that you can feel confident in all aspects of running your business, regardless of your natural strengths or current skillset.

HOW TO READ THIS BOOK

This book has ten chapters (Ten Basic Building Blocks), each covering a different aspect of business management. Then each chapter is further defined into sub-building blocks relevant to that topic. These elements form part of a giant jigsaw that helps you better understand your business as a whole.

This book references many **ABBREVIATIONS,** which are fully defined in the abbreviations sections at the end of the book.

In each chapter, key business terms are highlighted in bold and also fully explained in the **TERMINOLOGY** section at the end of the book.

It is a practical guide you can refer back to again and again as you continue to grow your business; not necessarily something you read from start to finish. Think of it more as a reference guide where you can dip into the sections you feel you need to learn the most.

Each chapter ends with a helpful set of "Healthcheck Questions" that reflect on what you've learned and how you can now apply it to your business. There are no right or wrong answers to these questions. I would encourage you to take the time to answer them honestly, as they will be extremely valuable in helping you grow your business.

So if you're feeling overwhelmed or like you're in over your head, don't worry! Just take it one chapter/question at a time, and I guarantee you will be surprised by how easy it can be to gain new perspectives, insights and ideas for your business.

WHAT YOU WILL LEARN

Rest reassured that it is never too late to go back and get the basics right. Sometimes, what seems like a step backwards can jolt your business forward.

The learning, insights and questions in this book will help you better understand the following areas:

- How to get finance and non-finance departments on the same page;
- How to build solid operations and a strong foundation for the company, from top-down and bottom-up;
- How to improve the communication and data flow within each team and inter-departmentally;
- How to understand your business processes from a different perspective;
- How to map out processes for much-improved customer and employee experience;
- How to increase the business's bottom line and improve your margins overall, by product line/customer and through waste reduction and not necessarily cutting headcount;
- How to increase teamwork and improve morale by understanding your people and business from a new perspective;
- How to automate your accounts team by implementing an easy-to-use **ACCOUNTING PACKAGE:** a system used to manage the financial activities of a company;
- How to train employees to have a growth mindset and look out for continuous improvement – for example, automate processes to avoid manual entry, prevent duplication of work, avoid duplicate payments and improve communications;
- How to ensure compliance with government regulations;

MY STORY

I grew up in Bawnree, Carlow, Ireland, "the middle of nowhere", as we call it. I am one of 10 children, and as a timid child, there was always someone else to speak on my behalf. We went to school and mass, which was about it back then, and I was only ever in the "Big City" on school tours.

The first time I had to speak up for myself was when I was 17 years old and started college in Dublin to study **MANAGEMENT ACCOUNTANCY (CIMA).** I soon realised communication was my strong point, listening and asking questions. I have loved learning and studying various courses, including leadership, taxation, LEAN, train the trainer, project management, resilience, and much more.

At 20 years of age, an opportunity arose to temporarily live and work in London. From then on, I couldn't get enough of learning and exploring the world and was fortunate enough to relocate to the Cayman Islands at 24. I thrived in these new environments. That's a long time ago, but I have not stopped talking, and asking questions has become my nature. I found my voice.

I am now self-employed as a Business and Operations Specialist after 25 years of working with corporate and privately-owned companies within all business life stages (start-up, growth, and mature turnaround). I successfully led many ad-hoc projects, system implementation, supply chain development, cash flow, strategic business planning and grant applications in sectors as diverse as Manufacturing, Production, Financial Services, Distillery, Engineering and Retail.

Although finance is my background, I love to work in all business areas. I love working with different cultures and cross-functionally with all departments. I thrive on change and am passionate about unlocking people's potential.

My foundations are rooted in finance, accounting and bottom-line numbers, which have helped me realise my true passion; meeting people, working with people, helping them understand how they add value to their business and leading them to stress-free operations and organisations.

To further learn, and develop your business or private one-to-one consultations, contact me *via* my website **www.maryhayden.com** or LinkedIn **www.linkedin.com/in/maryhaydenbusinessoperations**

1: BUSINESS

"Work harder on yourself than you do on your business".

Jim Rohn

In this chapter, you will find answers to the following questions:

- Why is having a vision and business plan essential?
- Why is it necessary to be clear on your unique selling point?
- Why is it so critical to have all your staff adequately trained?
- Why having up-to-date information makes managing your business easier?
- Why must you follow revenue and government regulations?
- Why is it essential to be audit-ready?
- Do you know where your data is stored and who has access to this data?
- Why do you need to know about available funding opportunities and cash flow?

Figure 1: *Sub-Building Blocks for Foundations Chapter*

Getting the foundations right to help grow and keep your business on target is extremely important.

As a business owner, you are undoubtedly very passionate about your business and on a never-ending curve to strive for success. When you achieve your goals, you seek once again to further that success so that, at times, it can seem there is never an end in sight. You are focused on executing your strategy, and whether you are willing to take significant risks or want to focus on profit, you need to know the basics and the foundations to stay on track.

You know you cannot take your eye off the market or your competition. The market is continually changing. Customer needs are dynamic and evolving. There will always be a new and shinier model of your product or service. You want the latest innovations and most desirable offerings to come from you, and rightly so.

In this chapter, we go through some of the business basics and fundamental concepts that can accelerate your success when in place.

STRATEGIC THINKING

STRATEGIC THINKING is the process of thinking about and organizing your business operations in a way that will allow you to achieve your long-term goals.

Being strategic necessitates having a clear plan for the future. This plan lets you know exactly where you are going, how and when you will get there and where you are currently on that journey.

Being strategic doesn't necessarily mean you need to think like a strategist all the time. It is about your state of mind, mental processes, and inner thoughts. It's essential to be in a resourceful mental state, able to access the correct information to address your business challenges and foresee what is coming down the line.

Too often, business owners and managers think that being busy equates to high productivity levels. You cannot afford to get lost in the day-to-day detail of operating your business only to lose sight of the big picture.

Strategic thinking is about being goal-orientated, focusing on the right things at the right time and knowing your direction. Everything starts from there. A business's MISSION and VISION are some of the most undervalued parts of a company; they give direction and meaning to your strategic plan – ignore them at your peril.

The **MISSION** refers to "Why your Company Exists"?

The **VISION** relates to the "Long-Term Aspirations for your Business."

If you were to ask your employees about your company's mission and vision, what do you think they would say? Would they be able to articulate clearly where the business is heading and why that is important? Would they know and be excited about the part they play in that mission and vision?

You must be crystal clear on what your mission and vision for the company are and clearly and consistently communicate to everyone you employ. Your mission and vision for the company are the glue that holds everything together and keeps everyone focused and on track. At the core, your mission and vision answer the question of why you do what you do. They give your company purpose and are a bold declaration of your business's big picture.

Document your company's mission and vision and refer to it regularly. All strategic decisions and priorities in your business should come from and align with your vision and mission. Don't allow yourself or your teams to lose sight of why you started this business and what you ultimately want to achieve.

CONSIDER THESE QUESTIONS FOR YOUR BUSINESS

- ✓ What is the purpose of your business?
- ✓ Why did you start in business?
- ✓ What do you ultimately want to achieve?
- ✓ Why do you want to achieve this?
- ✓ Who can help you accomplish this?
- ✓ What skills do you require of yourself and your team?
- ✓ What are potential obstacles and workarounds?
- ✓ What are your strategic goals?

"If you don't stand for something, you will fall for everything".

Anon

BUSINESS PLAN

A business plan is a projection of where you see your business one to five years from now or however far ahead you want to look. It forms an integral part of your business strategy and is a tangible output of your vision and mission statements. It is important not to overthink the business plan, especially when starting your company. You want to outline the goals or **OBJECTIVES** of the business, how you will reach them and the timeframe for their achievement. When this is presented In a written document format, it's called a business plan.

A business plan is a critical document for any business. It outlines your company's goals and strategies and helps you track your progress over time. To secure funding from investors, you will need a well-written business plan, or it may simply help you stay on track. It's essential to have a realistic and well-thought-out business plan if you want your business to be successful.

Most business plans for start-ups will be written on a couple of pages. The primary purpose should never be forgotten: the business plan gives anyone who looks at it an overview of the business. This doesn't have to be complicated and should be relatively easy to read and understand. A business plan should be as attractive to a potential investor as possible. This means you will include your business's financial aspects and plan to create future profits. For example, show revenue In different revenue streams, show margins by category, and a breakdown of all expenses.

It also includes your strategy for growth in all areas of your business. If your company has strengths and opportunities, it is the place to identify and describe them. Usually, this is done by aligning your business analysis with extensive market research. Your company's budget should be directly aligned with the business plan.

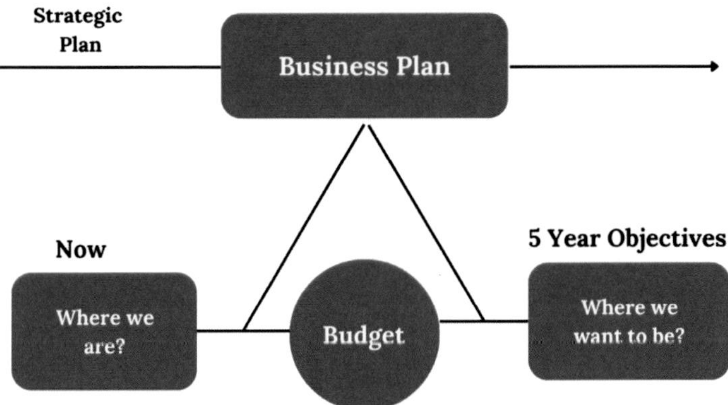

Figure 2: *Business Plan Diagram*

It's not necessary to overcomplicate your business plan. Please keep it simple, easy to understand and relevant to the current operating environment. For example, business plans for start-ups can be on two or three pages. If you haven't written a business plan before, here are some critical pieces of information to get you started:

- What is your Vision for the Business?
- The business Mission statement
- The unique selling point of your business
- An overview of your products and services
- What is the target market for your products and services
- How do you plan to reach your target market
- A description of your company structure and ownership
- An overview of your financial situation, including projected income and expenses
- A description of your marketing strategy
- An outline of your employee roles and responsibilities
- A description of your company's governance structure

If you want to be investor-ready, it's essential to have regular management accounts and historical data to back up future projections. A business plan should be as attractive to a potential investor as possible. This means that you should include all the financial aspects of your business and projections – data analysis that clearly shows the company's growth and future potential.

VALUES

Business values are a company owner's fundamental beliefs about what is essential for its operations. They guide the company's decisions and provide a compass for its actions. Values help to create a company culture and can be a significant factor in attracting and retaining employees. They can also be a key selling point when pitching to customers. Some of the most common business values include customer service, quality, innovation, teamwork, and integrity.

Values are important because they help to create a culture within a company. A strong culture based on shared values helps bind employees together. It also makes decision-making and action-taking easier when everyone aligns with what is important to the company. Finally, having values that align with the company's mission and vision sends a clear message to customers about what they can expect from doing business with you.

CONSIDER THESE QUESTIONS FOR YOUR BUSINESS

- ✓ What are your core values and belief systems?
- ✓ What values do you want for your company?
- ✓ What traits do you want to portray & have your company live up to?
- ✓ What do you stand for?
- ✓ What is okay and not okay regarding how you run your business?

Be crystal clear about your values. You are at the core pillar of your business, creating the epicentre around which everything spins. Therefore, it is vital to take a moment to ask some critical values-related questions.

You will run your business based on your values, so you want to surround yourself with people who understand and have similar values.

UNIQUE SELLING PROPOSITION

A **Unique Selling Proposition (USP)** is a statement that highlights the benefits a company offers that make it different from the competition. It is a vital element of any effective marketing strategy and can be used to create a competitive edge. When crafting a USP, it is crucial to focus on what makes your company stand out and why customers should choose you over the competition. The statement should be clear, concise, and easy to understand.

Business success starts with the product or service you are offering or planning to offer. You can have the best team globally, incredible amounts of **CAPITAL** (the total financial assets required to produce your goods or services), and the most willing market to place yourself in, but if you can't communicate your unique proposition; how your business is different, then none of the rest matters. It is helpful to start by asking yourself and your customers some fundamental questions about your product.

For example, many business owners can lose track of what problem their product or service is solving. They can go off on a tangent to improve the look and capability and lose sight of the original purpose. Marketing, sales, revenue models, and other aspects are all add-ons. You have to start with your product and ensure it is uniquely placed to solve a specific customer problem, ideally in a way no one else does.

Getting caught up in wanting to improve every other aspect of your business is easy. When you neglect the product, all your efforts are in vain. When it comes to the product, if your company fails to create something unique to solve its customers' problems, it may find it hard to retain those customers. You must understand what your customers want and what problems they want solved. Ask your customer for their feedback and get their opinions before investing time and money on a change or new product that may not sell.

These are the core questions that every potential customer wants to know about your business:

- What is your product?
- What is its differentiation or Unique Selling Point?
- What is its niche in the market?
- How are you innovating or adding value?
- What problem will your product solve for your customer?

CONSIDER THESE QUESTIONS FOR YOUR BUSINESS

✓ What problem are you solving for your customer?

✓ What makes your product or service different?

✓ What does your product do better than anyone else?

✓ How does it compare to your competitors?

✓ How does it add real value to someone who buys it?

Now that you know what your product is about and how it works, it is time to look at what makes it unique. Even if you don't have a differentiated, innovative or highly niched product, having a USP is necessary. Think about walking around in a market where many buyers have identical items. You might pass several stalls with the same product but will stop at the 10th one that offers you the same fruit as all the others.

What leads you to stop at this particular one? Most of the time, it is because something unique catches your attention. This uniqueness may be the friendly seller, how the items are displayed, or the stall owner's cute dog. Whatever it is, after passing several stalls, you stop at a certain one. There is something that catches your attention: something unique.

Too many businesses with high-quality products fail to communicate their uniqueness to potential prospects. It could be anything: speed, customer service, low cost, convenience, being the first, quality, willingness, friendliness, eagerness, or anything else that makes you different or allows you to stand out from the crowd.

To figure out your USP, you must ask yourself a fundamental question. Put yourself in the buyer's shoes and ask: "Why should the buyer buy from you and not from the competition?" You have to be able to answer this question with confidence!

VALUE ADD

Value-add goes hand in hand with your USP. There are many different ways your product can add value.

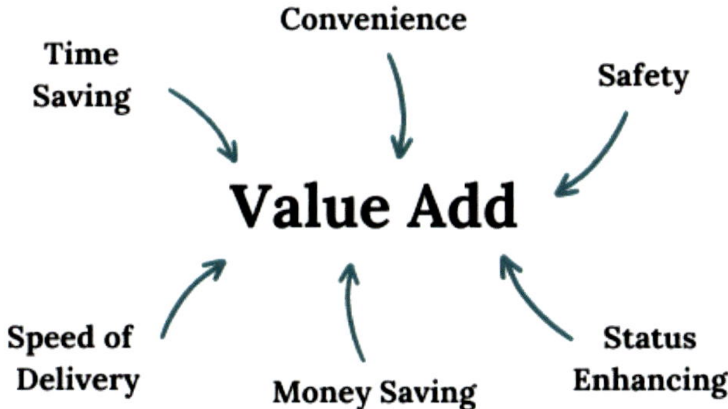

Figure 3: *Adding Value to your Business*

Traditionally, the value-add is how you can justify the difference between your product's cost and what you get in return. An example could be purchasing timber to make stairs. In this case, the value-add is the time and resources required to complete the stairs and how different they are from their competitors. How efficient is your process? What state-of-the-art equipment are you using? What specialist skills have your staff? What grade of timber do you use? What are the quality checks carried out? And so on.

In a more general sense, value-add is the value prospective clients perceive that your product has. Several factors come into play, each more attractive to different buyers (which we will discuss later).

Customers spend their money on a product or service to add value to their life. It sounds simple, but many businesses neglect this. You prove your product's worth when you convince your prospect to buy your product instead of a competitor's. If you are still struggling to find a value-add, the infographic above contains some examples.

You maybe already adding value and not realise it; ask your customers why they decided to buy from you and not your competition, and let them tell you how you are already adding value to them.

CUSTOMER

Who is your customer? Before you answer that question, know that "everyone" cannot be the answer. You cannot serve everyone's needs. Even though you can help a broad range of customers doesn't mean you should. When it comes to marketing your product or service, if you try to speak to "everyone", you will end up being heard by no one.

So the next step in building a solid business foundation is identifying who exactly your ideal customer is. You want to be as specific as possible to identify the customer.

CONSIDER THESE QUESTIONS FOR YOUR BUSINESS

- ✓ Who specifically is your target market?
- ✓ What are the specific traits of your ideal customer?
- ✓ What problems, goals, and aspirations do they have?
- ✓ What do they want from you?
- ✓ Do you have a narrow focus or a broad range of ideas?
- ✓ How could becoming more niche add to your bottom line?

Now you might be asking yourself, "why should I focus only on a certain number of buyers if I could target the whole market?" The answer lies in the question. Everyone has different needs and problems. These can be categorised and even subcategorised. The more specific you identify an issue of a particular target market, the better.

Narrowing your focus and knowing your niche and customer is one of the most effective strategies for improving your bottom line. By limiting your service type or product mix and the projects you accept, you can be more productive and produce higher-quality output.

INNOVATION

Innovation can be intimidating, but it doesn't need to be, and you don't have to change the world to make innovation a constant companion in your business. **INNOVATION** means adding and/or improving current products/services or continually looking for more reliable, cheaper, and consistent improvements to your current offerings. Regardless of how small you think it is, every aspect of your business counts. Even the slightest improvement at one point could lead to massive improvements down the line.

CONSIDER THESE QUESTIONS FOR YOUR BUSINESS

- ✓ Where can you improve?
- ✓ What can you do differently?
- ✓ How else could your product look or behave?
- ✓ How else can you deliver your service?
- ✓ Where are opportunities to stand out even more?

To be innovative does not only mean continuously looking at how you can reinvent the wheel. Sometimes, you have to look at a process and ask yourself how you could do it differently. Maybe the old saying if it's not broke, don't fix it, needn't apply to your business.

For example, a car might not be broken, but it's worth looking at if you can get another 100km per charge. We can quickly get stuck in a rut of routine, accepting things just the way they are, not challenging the *status quo*.

Create an innovation mindset in your business by asking questions and consistently striving for improvements, no matter how small. By asking what you can do differently, you might open up new pathways to improve existing products, reduce costs, and improve your bottom line.

QUALITY

Everyone wants quality, whether in the form of an experience, a product or a service. Focusing on quality leads to repeat business through referrals, saving you time and money on advertising.

Customers talking about how great it is to do business with you is the best recommendation you can get! You maintain your old, satisfied customers and get new ones. Having a reputation for high-quality offerings also means you can charge higher prices. This price increase will result in increased revenue and a healthier bottom line.

And remember, improving the quality of your business doesn't necessarily have to cost you money! In fact, identifying efficiencies, improving the customer experience and introducing digital transformation can lead to higher quality and a cost reduction for your business. Win-win!

CONSIDER THESE QUESTIONS FOR YOUR BUSINESS

- ✓ What in your business do you do well?
- ✓ Is there any room for improvement?
- ✓ Do you capture and analyse customer feedback?
- ✓ What are your most common customer complaints?
- ✓ Are there quality-related sources of inspiration you can get from other industries or sectors?

If you're not sure where to start with quality improvements, the first place to go is to your customer enquiries and complaints. Ask your customers for feedback and suggestions. Your customers are the best source of where improvements can be made in your business. Keep your customer close, listen to what they say, and you can never fail to go wrong.

COMPLIANCE

Compliance means adhering to a set of government regulations and guidelines. Laws are in place to ensure that businesses operate fairly and ethically, protect consumers, and maintain the economy's stability. Compliance can be costly and time-consuming, but it is necessary for your business's survival and success.

You must ensure that all your staff are trained adequately on compliance policies and procedures and that you have up-to-date information on relevant regulations. You must also follow revenue and government regulations and be audit-ready.

When completing the healthcheck questions at the end of this chapter, consider the compliance guidelines for each function within your business.

Compliance is never a problem until it is, and by then, it is often too late. Lack of compliance can result in significant setbacks in your business, so ensuring you stay compliant should be high in your priorities. Think Revenue, Health and Safety, Food Hygiene, Employee Relations, Environment and Quality.

You want to consider compliance elements in all processes and for all decision-making. I will cover some critical aspects of this in later chapters.

If compliance is something you haven't focused on to date, I suggest you start with your business's **HEALTH & SAFETY (H&S)** processes and procedures. It is a vital topic! Not just ensuring the health and safety of your employees but also your customers, vendors and other business partners. Be proactive and conduct an H&S audit on your business or get outside help if you don't have the resources to do one on your own.

Investing the time and money to do this now could save you a fortune (or a lawsuit) later down the line.

Another quick win when it comes to compliance is documentation. A common adage in the corporate world is "if it's not documented, it's not done", but most businesses neglect documentation because it is time-consuming.

However, having documented processes and procedures can make it easier for employees to follow compliance-related topics and be a lifeline when audited. The same documentation can benefit staff training, up-skilling and ensuring knowledge isn't lost when an employee leaves the business.

Depending on your industry, you may need to consider other governing bodies, like the **ENVIRONMENTAL PROTECTION AGENCY (EPA)**. Are all duties carried out in line with EPA requirements? What rivers, houses, and industries are in your area? What pollutants does your company use?

And another hot compliance topic relates to **Green Business or Sustainability**. How sustainable is your business? Consider efficiency in your operations, eco-consciousness, recycling, a paper-free environment, and reusing paper. How can your company be more Green? What renewable energy options do you have?

CONCLUSION

I hope by now you can see ways to strengthen the foundations of your company, and by the time to get to the end of this book, you will be even clearer on your product or service, how you want to deliver it and be more precise on whom exactly you want to provide it to.

Are there areas of improvement in your business? What are the challenge areas? Is there chaos at times? What does chaos in your business mean? And how is it created?

There are many reasons why parts of a business can spiral out of control. For example, inconsistent recruitment, lack of innovation, or employees not being motivated to deal with an increased workload can be detrimental to your company's future growth but can be alleviated entirely when you continuously focus on getting the basics right.

Issues can also arise if your staff don't understand or work with your belief system or values. Too few staff can lead to high turnover, low morale or burnout. If staff don't understand the company's long-term vision, they may make the wrong decisions. Then you lose time by being reactive to problems instead of proactive and forward-thinking; avoid this by including staff and asking them for suggestions. Their insights will be invaluable, ensuring they know their support and tips are welcome and valuable.

Overspending can lead to cash flow issues. Being too busy with all the day-to-day problems can lead to a loss of clients. Even "just" thinking of short-term revenue instead of engaging with customers, new products, or markets can lead to a loss of market share.

Automation is another area of importance for your business. Is there an element of manual work? Can this be automated? Are there simple daily day-to-day tasks that will save time and ensure more accurate data if the process is automated? More detail on that in upcoming chapters. And as we dive deeper into each topic, I will help guide you by posing questions that will trigger insights about where you might be in your business and how you can improve.

FOUNDATIONS HEALTHCHECK

1. Do I know what my vision, mission and values are?

2. What Is the Unique Selling Point of my product or service?

3. What value am I adding to the customer?

4. Who is my target customer? (be specific!)

5. Am I actively pursuing innovation or constant improvement?

6. Am I offering a quality product?

7. Am I seeking new markets?

8. Do I have access to a Business Plan or Budget?

9. What are my Quality Standards, and are they measured?

10. Do I practice continuous improvement?

NOTES

2: INFORMATION

"Most people spend more time and energy going around problems than trying to solve them".

Henry Ford

In this chapter, you will find answers to the following questions:

- What are the critical components of information management and compliance?
- How should you manage the information and data held by your company?
- Why might you need an **ENTERPRISE RESOURCE PLANNING (ERP)** system?
- What do you need to know about **BUSINESS INTEGRATION**?
- What are the essentials related to employee data access, management and controls?
- How **LEAN** and continuous improvement approaches are applied to information management?
- What do you need to know about Business **WASTE**?

Figure 4: *Sub-Building Blocks for Information Management*

There is lots of information available in any business, and managing this information is vital. For a company to stay competitive, it needs systems to collect and analyse the data. Additionally, companies must comply with government regulations, industry data access, and storage.

The types of information collected and analyzed come in many forms:

- Financial data
- Customer data
- Inventory data
- Production data, and
- Marketing data

Now more than ever, information management has become a hot topic, particularly with the increase in remote working triggered by the COVID-19 pandemic. Virtual meetings are now the norm and have had tremendous business benefits, like reducing the need for travel expenses.

Virtual offices have eliminated the need for physical space, so the monthly office rental bill could be removed entirely if that made sense for your business. However, it has also presented new challenges regarding data access, protection and security of customer and business information. Having effective **MANAGEMENT INFORMATION SYSTEMS (MIS**) tools in place ensures that you can balance the benefits of remote working with the risks that can come from remote system access to critical business data.

INFORMATION

Management information systems (MIS) refers to the relationship between people and technology in your organisation. You want to maximise the benefit of your investment in employees, equipment and business processes. MIS is people orientated as much as technology-based; it provides the best service through better technology and **STREAMLINED** business processes. It relates to the process of collecting, organizing, storing, retrieving, and disseminating information in a business.

The main goal of MIS is to help managers make informed decisions. The most important part of MIS is the information it provides to managers. With accurate and timely information, managers can make strategic decisions to help their businesses grow and succeed.

Within your business, each employee is responsible for managing information for their position or carrying out their duties, including where to store, find and analyse this data. The system and information collected will differ depending on the user, management, staff or customer.

For example, a customer service representative will access customer contact data, recent enquiries or complaints, and billing information for purchased products by customers. A member of your Human Resources (HR) team will access employee data, emergency contacts, salary and compensation packages and performance management data.

We want to ensure that your employees can access the information they need to do their jobs effectively. This information also needs to be secure, accurate and offered in the best format for the user.

CONSIDER THESE QUESTIONS FOR YOUR BUSINESS

- ✓ What information do my employees need access to do their jobs effectively?
- ✓ What information is considered confidential or requires additional levels of security?
- ✓ Where is data stored – physically or on a system?
- ✓ Is it Cloud or Server-Based?
- ✓ Is it backed up, how often, and where is the backup stored?
- ✓ Who has access (user access rights) to the information and the locations on the Cloud, One Drive, or Google Drive?
- ✓ How can I stop data from being downloaded or removed from the business, e.g. on a USB?

Information can be collected, processed, and stored in several ways at all levels of **OPERATIONS** within your business. Every decision you make is based on the information you receive. It then makes sense for you to set up systems to collect and store critical data to ensure better decision-making at all levels of your business.

Such systems include accounting packages, footfall counters, point of sale information, inventory tracking, sales information, **DASHBOARDS**, and so much more. An up-to-date live information system analysis will help your business reach its goals and give you a competitive advantage over other companies.

A lack of up-to-date information can cause a business to have an inaccurate view of what is happening and can lead to bad decisions.

How can you realistically make the right decision if you don't have access to the correct information?

DATA ACCESS

Data access is one of the main components of a data governance programme in an organisation. Data is just another word for information. When you review data access within your company, you will want to know who has access to what information. Are user rights tracked and documented? Can this user access be quickly reviewed and amended? Are their audit trails in place?

CONSIDER THESE QUESTIONS FOR YOUR BUSINESS

- ✓ Who has access to what data?
- ✓ Do they need to have access to it?
- ✓ How readily available and accessible is your data?
- ✓ Where is this information stored?
- ✓ How often do you change passwords, and who has access?

Anything that can be measured and recorded is regarded as data. Any activity within the business that can be recorded and reviewed is essentially data. Many companies have hit the news because of unexpected data breaches and leaks, so you can see why it's essential to know who has access to what information and controls to manage it.

The first step is to nominate someone to control the company's information. It might be a department manager, the IT department, the information owner or human resources. If your business is of a specific size, you may even have a dedicated Chief Data Officer (this has now become the norm in many organisations since the introduction of the General Data Protection Regulation).

A data breach can have profound negative implications on a business. In the event of compromised customer or client data, the company could face legal action from those affected. Additionally, a data breach can damage a company's reputation, resulting in a loss of customers and revenue. Finally, the cost of repairing the damage caused by a data breach can be considerable. As such, it is critical for businesses to protect their data and quickly and effectively respond in the event of a violation.

Simple processes can make a big difference and protect your business from data access issues. Take for example "garden leave".

"Garden leave" refers to when an employee is paid for their notice period but doesn't have to work. There are many reasons that employers have to use garden leave. Garden leave is essential if the employee works in a highly confidential department with an opportunity to leak confidential/personal information. It can seem very cold, especially if employees have been with the company for several years. However, every company has the right and responsibility to protect its data.

This process is not personal but an acceptable policy to have in place to protect company data. This is also an excellent reason to write up procedures and documentation of the roles within your business. You may need to exit an employee quickly, resulting in no proper handover. Employees may have to leave last minute for many different reasons. At least with some procedures to follow, a new employee has a starting point, and the company doesn't lose out.

Additionally, when an employee leaves your company, remember to delete all their system access and change relevant passwords. This is more important now than ever, with remote working and employees having access to work via personal computers, phones and other devices.

These kinds of challenges lead nicely to the topic of the **GENERAL DATA PROTECTION REGULATION (GDPR)**, a new EU data protection law enacted on May 25, 2018. The GDPR replaces the 1995 EU Data Protection Directive. It strengthens EU data protection rules by giving individuals more control over their data and establishing new rights for individuals.

Under the GDPR, all organizations that process the personal data of EU citizens must comply with a set of core principles concerning how personal data must be collected, processed, and stored. These principles are known as the "GDPR requirements."

Organizations that process the personal data of EU citizens must also appoint a Data Protection Officer (DPO), implement risk management processes and establish an incident response plan. They must also ensure that individuals have a right to receive information about their data rights and access to their data.

Organizations that process the personal data of EU citizens must also contact individuals about any rectification or erasure requests they make and must provide individuals with a copy of their data upon request. Finally, organizations must ensure that individuals have the right to complain if they believe there is a violation of their rights.

CONSIDER THESE QUESTIONS FOR YOUR BUSINESS

- ✓ What information do you gather as a business?
- ✓ How and where is that information stored, and for how long?
- ✓ Do you have processes for customers to request access to their data?
- ✓ Do you have a public statement on your controls related to information handling?
- ✓ Do employees have information on personal laptops, company laptops or phones?
- ✓ Do they understand GDPR and have the proper training to process data securely?

SYSTEM INTEGRATION

SYSTEM or **BUSINESS INTEGRATION** (BI) is where you combine information from one or more systems to have better overall information. By doing so, businesses can improve communication and data sharing among departments, making tracking and analysing business performance easier. SI can also help companies to integrate new technologies more quickly and easily, which gives them a competitive edge in the marketplace.

If you are considering systems integration for your business, I recommend you undertake a detailed analysis of your needs to ensure you will get a good return on your investment. This analysis should include an assessment of the business's current processes and systems and an evaluation of the gaps between them and what is needed to support your business's strategic objectives; only after the completion of the assessment should a business look into potential systems integrators and begin negotiating contracts.

Undoubtedly, even the simplest of integrations can quickly benefit a business, customers and employees. I mentioned earlier that MIS uses technology and information to help employees do their job effectively and stay on task. For example, timesheets or time management systems can enable employees to track their time usage: time spent on different work activities, projects or billable hours for invoicing. Integrating time management and finance systems can simplify the business's necessary billing, payment and performance management processes.

CONSIDER THESE QUESTIONS FOR YOUR BUSINESS

- ✓ How are processes carried out currently?
- ✓ Can any process be improved or changed?
- ✓ Can any element be automated?
- ✓ Why is this task carried out?
- ✓ What is the system flow of information, manual *vs* automated?
- ✓ Are you gathering information in one place and using it in more than one department?
- ✓ In what format is data collected?
- ✓ How do you integrate this data?
- ✓ Is there manual input and room for human error?
- ✓ Is information audited for completeness or accuracy?
- ✓ What Systems can you integrate?

ENTERPRISE RESOURCE PLANNING

Another term often heard in the business world is **ENTERPRISE RESOURCE PLANNING (ERP)**. ERP refers to a software package to align the business or manage the entire supply chain's business processes. ERP is a part of the broader MIS process, but many other tools are part of MIS. If your business is at the growth stage or has reached current capacity levels with resources, you may feel the need to implement or purchase an ERP system.

ERP aligns information from across the operations; for example, Finance, Personnel, Production, Sales, Supply Chain, Customer Relationship Management (CRM) and Project Management. Below I have highlighted some of the information that may be monitored and contained in an ERP:

- **Finance:** accounting, loans, payments, cost management, cash flow, budgeting, analysis, taxation, intercompany consolidation;
- **Personnel:** onboarding, recruiting, training, payroll;
- **Production:** purchase orders, warehousing, equipment costs, materials, and production facilities, stock control, operations, production and quality, after-sales service;
- **Sales:** pricing, ordering, and processing, sales analysis, products, markets;

- **Supply chain:** planning, purchasing, inventory, product configurations, handling claims;
- **Project management:** resource planning and usage, costing, billing, and management;
- **CRM:** marketing, sales, customer service, fees, contact management, workflow maintenance.

ERP simplifies essential business routines or processes and provides information for analysis and decision-making. It prevents the duplication of data and unifies management cross-functionally. It allows for growth within companies with access to data for decision-making, letting managers know what areas to concentrate on or eliminate.

It's essential to repeat that an ERP is only part of an MIS. It doesn't solve all issues or information flow, nor does it eliminate all waste. Increased communication and overall efficiency within the company are required to achieve growth. Managers must also take responsibility for information systems and ensure they manage and communicate effectively regarding what they ultimately want to achieve. The ERP chosen must be compatible with current information systems and any other business platforms (software or hardware) already used by the business.

CONSIDER THESE QUESTIONS FOR YOUR BUSINESS

- ✓ Do you need an ERP?
- ✓ When is a good time to consider this investment?
- ✓ How will ERP improve your business?
- ✓ What are your main challenges?
- ✓ How can you improve them?
- ✓ What will the Return On Investment ROI be?

Purchasing ERP may involve a one-off hardware and software investment but may also have an ongoing annual licence and support costs. Consider Cloud-based systems as they can reduce the up-front fee in return for a monthly/yearly subscription.

One of the main advantages of an ERP system is access to the master files. e.g. when a new customer comes on board, their information is entered into the system. Therefore you won't have to ask for it again, and you know where to find it for ease of access.

The same applies to new employees, suppliers, products and projects. Information is collected once and built upon, and therefore there is less risk of data loss as the system will be backed up, with less manual work, duplication and errors; the focus can be on the customers rather than manual data collection, allowing you to provide a more efficient service.

Regardless of the investment cost of an ERP, it can pay off quickly, meeting your business needs, providing efficiencies and allowing your company to grow. There are many different ERP platforms, most with similar functionality. Some of the most popular ones on the market today (in no particular order) are:

- SAP Business One
- SAP ERP
- SAGE
- Microsoft Dynamics Business 365 Business Central
- Oracle NetSuite
- Enterpryze

LEAN / CONTINUOUS IMPROVEMENT

The term **LEAN** is used in connection with **CONTINUOUS IMPROVEMENT (CI).** CI relates to any improvement in a company, big or small, to improve the customer journey and the value of the product or service provided to the customer.

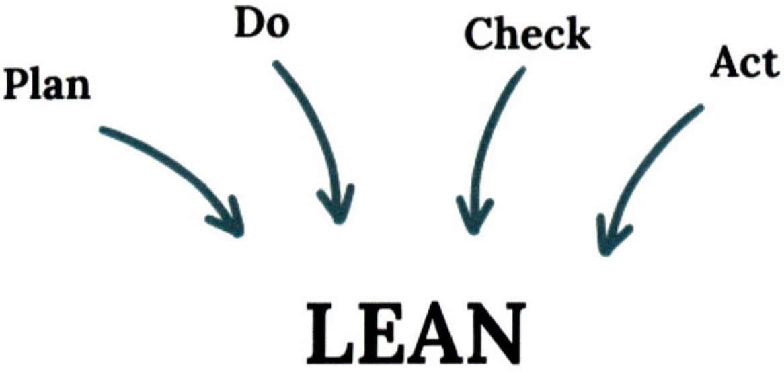

Figure 5: *Continuous Improvement*

The goal is that all employees have the mindset to improve and make minor tweaks to work more efficiently. Employees must have access to the data they require to carry out their duties, know where to access it, and prevent them from wasting time looking for the information they need to carry out their duties.

It's vital that you know where your company is now, "Current State," *versus* where you want it to go, "Future State". With this future vision, you can set up systems, processes and business integration to improve efficiency. It can be particularly beneficial to map out the customer journey; easy-to-use tools are available to help with this, including **Value Stream Mapping (VSM)**, Process Mapping, and Flow Charts.

There are many, many LEAN tools – a subject for another book! For now, all you need to think about is the minor tweaks you and your employees can make to allow for continuous improvement and, ultimately, improve the product and service to the customer and add to the bottom line.

WASTE

The good news is that we can make huge efficiencies with simple tweaks in our daily processes and procedures. Kiichiro Toyoda, the founder of Toyota Motor Corporation, firmly believed in the philosophy that "the ideal conditions for making things are created when machines, facilities, and people work together to add value without generating any **WASTE**".

Waste is not necessarily just what you throw in the bin. Waste in business refers to any obsolete materials or stock, but it also relates to any inefficiencies or inaccuracies within your business that produce a less-than-optimal result. The Japanese LEAN term for waste is MUDA which means futility or idleness. Waste is also referred to by the acronym TIMWOODS (Transport, Inventory, Motion, Waste, Overprocessing, Overproduction, Defects and Skills). This acronym is used to easily remember and identify the eight wastes that apply to any industry. Waste management is vital to ensure you get the best value and maximum return for your materials, products, processes, and even people.

Look at the eight types of waste and think about your business. Where is the waste in your business? Get your employees involved in this process for their respective areas. The aim is not only to look out for harmful elements but to look at ways of improving the overall operations.

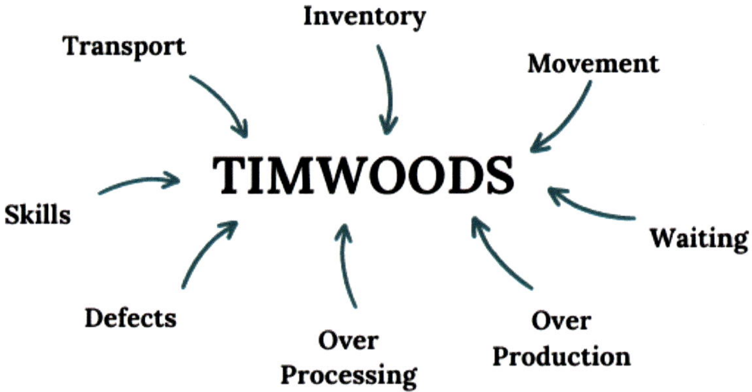

Figure 6: *TIM WOOD – 8 Types of Waste*

For example:

- What are your business goals?
- Do you have a system to track your progress towards your goals?
- What are the main obstacles to achieving your goals?
- Where might there be waste in your internal systems or processes?
- What management information can you access to identify waste and opportunities for improvement?

We often hear the phrase, *"what gets measured gets done"*, and I one hundred per cent believe that to be true. Without management information systems and processes, critical business and employee performance are unmanaged. Unfortunately, most employees will become less productive when specific performance elements are not measured or managed closely. When you measure an output, you can manage it, track it and improve it!

CONSIDER THESE QUESTIONS FOR YOUR BUSINESS

- ✓ What data do you capture?
- ✓ Why is that data necessary?
- ✓ Which data are you not capturing?
- ✓ Could you implement data-capturing software?
- ✓ What metrics can help you measure the waste?
- ✓ How can you eliminate waste?

CONCLUSION

You can see now that it is necessary to have systems and processes for as many of your business activities as possible. These systems and processes benefit everyone involved in the business, as well as your customers, but remember that you shouldn't set them in stone. The market you operate in is dynamic; your customer needs are changing, so your systems and processes should be as agile as your business needs.

Most business owners have a lot to consider regarding information management and how best to use it in their business. How can you tell if you are straying off the path if you don't have systems or processes to monitor your data or measure your performance? Systems and processes will guide your decision-making and keep you on track with your objectives and business goals.

"Data is becoming the New Raw Material for Business."

Craig Mundie: Senior Advisor to CEO at Microsoft

INFORMATION MANAGEMENT HEALTHCHECK

1. What information do I gather, and for what purpose?
2. What Information Technology Systems do I have or do I need?
3. Are all employees appropriately trained on secure data handling and other data topics, e.g. Cyber Security?
4. Do I have GDPR-compliant processes in place?
5. Would my business benefit from an ERP System?
6. Can I identify and reduce waste by improving my systems?
7. What information management policies do I have in place?
8. How am I currently carrying out my business? How could I do it differently?
9. Are our processes documented and kept up to date?
10. Can I improve on tasks or streamline some processes?

NOTES

3: CUSTOMERS

"You've got to start with the customer experience and work back toward the technology – not the other way around".

Steve Jobs

In this chapter, you will find answers to the following questions:

- Why is it essential to know your customer?
- Why is it necessary to understand what your customer wants?
- Why is it important to hire people with the right attitude?
- Why is it so vital to meet customers in person?
- Why do you need to improve your product continuously?
- Why are your quality levels critical to long-term success?

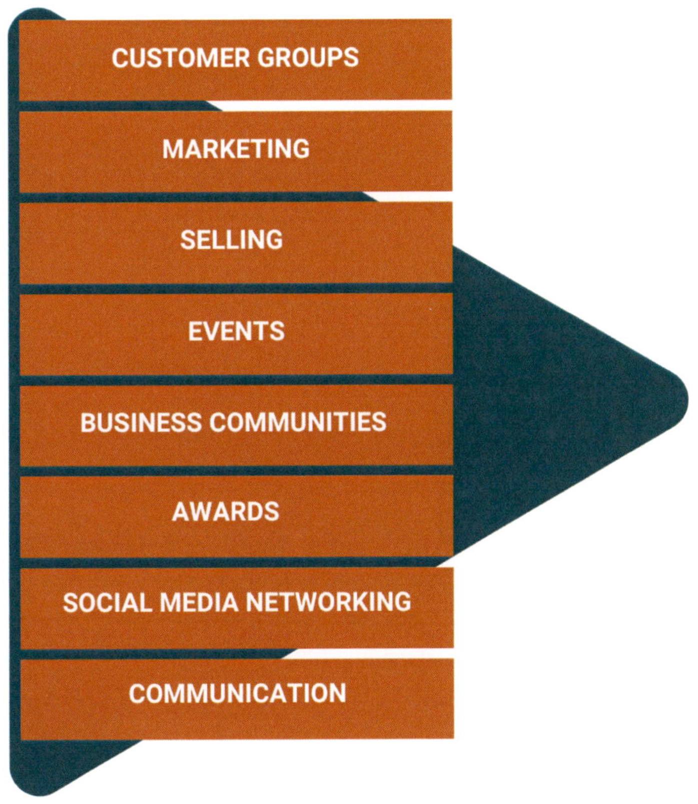

Figure 7: *Sub-Building Blocks for Customers*

Customers are the lifeblood of any business. To succeed, you must clearly understand who your customers are. Understanding the customer includes understanding what they need and want, what form of communication they like, and what motivates them to buy from you.

Once you know this, you can start to build a relationship with them and provide them with the products or services they're looking for. You'll have difficulty succeeding in business if you don't know your customers.

Think about it this way: if you're selling products or services, you need to know your target market. Otherwise, you're just shooting in the dark and hoping that something will stick. It's much better to take the time to understand your customer's unique needs and preferences to provide them with precisely what they need.

I also mentioned earlier that not every customer is the same - they are all motivated by different things. Customers' unique motivation influences their decision to buy something or look for an alternative. Even if you are an experienced seller, making a sale with a client will be easier and faster when you know what type of customer you are dealing with, their preferences, and their potential objections.

In short, knowing your customer is essential to any business's success. Without this knowledge, you'll struggle to build relationships, create a loyal customer base, and ultimately achieve your business goals. So take the time to learn about them - I promise it'll be worth it in the long run.

CUSTOMER

When we speak about the Customer, we are talking to three different types of customers:

- The **Internal Customer** refers to your employees;
- The **External Customer** is the person (or business) who will purchase your products or services
- The **Stakeholders** are also your customer and are considered in decision-making. They are interested in its financial standing: e.g. banks, board of directors, or Investors.

Each customer type has different needs and expectations that we must meet. Your employees' expectations will differ from those of your customers and/or stakeholders. And even within each type, you can have various sub-categories or segments that will dictate how you communicate with and support them.

For example, the External Customer can be further segmented:

- Prospective Customer
- New Customer
- Loyal Customer
- Returning Customer
- Churned Customer

Figure 8: *Three Customer Types*

It is definitely worth spending some time mapping out the customer types for your business. Identify their specific needs and expectations. Even better, map out a Customer Journey for each (you get an A+ for doing that)! Get your employees, stakeholders and even your customers involved in brainstorming ideas or conducting additional research. This mapping is valuable content that can inform future marketing and customer experience strategies for your business.

CUSTOMER GROUPS

We also need to touch on the different types of Customer groups because this can add insight when considering your external customers. There are five distinct groups detailed below:

- **Impulsive buyers** are people who, without much information, act on emotion rather than knowledge. These need minimal convincing, and there is usually very little following up that needs to be done. Experience shows that an impulsive buyer will be less likely to feel buyer's remorse or complain about the product after the purchase. Here it is wise to act on positive emotion rather than on technical details;
- **Technical buyers** are not as easily convinced with a big smile as impulsive buyers. Technical buyers are only interested in a product or service's technological advantages and details. The niceties of polite conversations are not vital to them; they want to get straight to why your product is the best option. It can be helpful to have your most technical employee with you to help with any questions this type of buyer may ask. Do not expect to make the sale after the first meeting. A technical buyer will weigh up other options before making their decision;
- **Conservative buyers** are much like technical buyers, without going into every product detail. They are less interested in your product's technical details and instead focus on the quality of the product. An example may be someone who replaces their car every 20 years but will not decide on the price. Here it is crucial to build a relationship and convince them that you will be there for any needs, even when the sale is complete;
- **Money savers**, or penny pinchers, are all about the product price. If your quality is acceptable, and your price is even a fraction cheaper than your competitor's, you will have the sale immediately. Money savers share the emotional aspect of the impulsive buyer. When customers see the money-saving, they will immediately make the purchase. This Impulse buying does not mean that they do not care about quality, but the price is the primary determining factor;
- The "**1%ers**" of buyers relate to the customer who does not care about price or quality but is looking to make a purchase right now. They are looking for a specific product, and if you are the one to speak to them first, they will go with your offering. They need little convincing and little follow-up. They only make up an estimated 1% of total buyers. But it is good practice to market your products to a broad range of prospects for visibility.

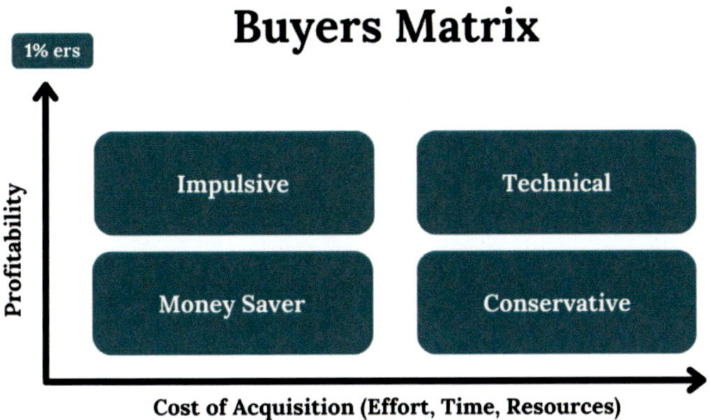

Figure 9: *The Buyers Matrix*

MARKETING

Marketing is the process of creating awareness and demand for a product or service. Marketing is important because it helps businesses reach new customers, build brand awareness, and drive sales. Without marketing, businesses would struggle to survive.

There are many different aspects to marketing, and it can be challenging to know where to start. However, understanding marketing basics is essential for any business owner or manager. We can divide Marketing into four main areas:

- Advertising and Promotion
- Public Relations
- Market Research
- Product Sales

Advertising and promotion are essential tools for creating awareness and demand for a product or service. They can be used to reach new customers and build brand awareness.

Public relations is another important aspect of marketing. Public relations can help businesses build relationships with the media, customers, and other stakeholders. It can also help businesses manage their reputation.

Market research is essential for understanding the needs and wants of customers. Market research can help businesses develop new products and services to help them understand what customers think of their current offerings.

Sales is the process of selling products or services to customers. Sales is important because it helps businesses generate revenue and grow.

The underlying question you need to consider regarding your marketing strategy is how you will ensure that your target market are aware of your product.

- Where will you advertise your product?
- What online and offline channels will you use?
- Where are your customers most likely to find you?
- What do your promotions need to look and sound like to attract the attention of your target audience?
- How can you make your marketing unique and memorable?

There are two distinct approaches when considering how you will market your product. As the word suggests, this refers to the kind of "market" you are entering.

The first consideration is to identify how broad your audience is. You may decide it is best to cover as much ground with your marketing as possible. As mentioned above, this is advantageous if you are unsure who your ideal buyer is. This is also a good approach if you want to experiment with the reaction of potentially new target audiences and types of customers. For example, you might advertise as a gym that serves anyone who wants to work out.

The second approach is to market only to a select and niche group of prospective buyers. This approach is advantageous when you have specific pre-identified needs of potential customers. You know your target audience, their pain points and their needs and can create a campaign that speaks directly to them. An example is a gym that advertises weight loss and fitness classes for new mothers who have just had their babies, men over 60 years old, or another target audience.

It's also important to note that marketing does not always equate to requiring a massive budget. With the rise of **SOCIAL MEDIA** advertising, companies can grow their audiences "organically" with little to no investment. **ORGANIC GROWTH** is a marketing strategy that creates naturally shareable content and promotes word-of-mouth marketing. This type of content is usually informative, entertaining, or both. It attracts attention and encourages people to share it with their social networks. Organic growth aims to build a brand presence and generate leads without spending any money on advertising.

SELLING

As a business owner, selling is one of the most important things you can do to ensure the success of your business. When done correctly, selling brings in new customers, grows your revenue, and helps you achieve your business goals. However, selling is not always easy, and it takes practice to become good at it.

I work with many business owners who tell me they are not effective salespeople or that they can't sell at all. In reality, every person has the ability to sell, but there can be some negative connotations related to not wanting to be "salesy" or "pushy". Some of the best "sellers" I have met are business owners who are passionate about their products or service. Their excitement about what they offer can be contagious and always comes across positively to any potential customer. There is nothing more attractive than genuine, heartfelt passion for a product.

I believe everyone is a salesperson, even if unbeknownst to themselves. And it isn't just extroverted people who make the best salespeople because of their talkative nature. I have seen extreme introverts sell a product better than their department's best salesperson. Selling is the ability to convince someone that they want your product. That is why many business owners can be very persuasive when selling their ideas and products to big companies; because they know their product inside and out, they can easily articulate its benefits and all the reasons why a customer should have it.

Apart from that, it is good to have a few guiding principles. Watch any movie about business, and you will see a salesperson shouting, "**ALWAYS BE CLOSING (ABC)**". This type of selling is known as "The ABC of Selling". It's true because you are in business to sell and not make friends, but creating a good relationship and putting your customer needs first will complete the transaction much easier with organic growth and improved brand reputation. ABC is a handy little framework to rely on when meeting potential customers or networking in general.

It is also essential to not just talk about your product and what it does right from the start. Asking a few questions about your potential customer's needs might uncover a whole new "in" for your product. If you can identify the customer's real needs and offer them a solution, you will already have a head start. This is true, even when compared to the most attractive and charismatic salesperson. That is why it is imperative to start by asking questions, paying close attention and then identifying how you can be the cure for their itch!

CONSIDER THESE QUESTIONS FOR YOUR BUSINESS

- ✓ What problems can you solve for the customer?
- ✓ What is the solution they are looking for?
- ✓ How and where do your customers prefer to buy?
- ✓ What are their potential objections?
- ✓ How and what have they already heard about you?
- ✓ How can your sales processes be improved?

EVENTS

Event marketing and networking are both great ways to promote your business. Event marketing can help you raise awareness for your brand and get people interested in what you offer. Networking can also help you connect with potential customers and clients and build relationships with other businesses in your industry. Use these strategies together to create a well-rounded marketing plan to help you reach your target audience and achieve your business goals.

I feel strongly that nothing will ever replace the importance of face-to-face interaction with customers. As humans, we are driven to have personal connections with other people. And you will want to connect with your target audience and plant your brand in their minds. Do this both on and offline. Online has become more popular due to the COVID-19 pandemic. More customers than ever now prefer to shop online. But there are still opportunities to cultivate customer relationships and marketing via multiple channels. Knowing how and where your customers prefer to connect can be a great source of inspiration for designing events and curating unique experiences.

Many community groups, business associations and industry bodies host events. You can leverage these valuable forums to increase your company's visibility and share what you do. You often hear the phrase, "people buy people first and then the product". Spread the word about your brand face-to-face, and connect with people. They will then spread it further for you or connect you with influencers who can open new channels. You might also find future business partners, suppliers or prospective customers.

Sales at networking events can be a bit tricky. The attendees are often there to meet others, build their network and gain knowledge and the last thing you want is to try to sell to someone who doesn't want to be sold to. However, this does not mean you can't discuss what you do and how you do it. I would advise that you focus more on sharing your story than focusing on making a sale. Give people a chance to get to know you, like you and trust you. Even getting someone's contact details so you can continue building the relationship after an event is a win.

If it is your event or if you are a speaker, then you are an experienced professional. All you have to do is socialise with the people at the event and answer any questions they might ask as if it is the most important question ever. After that, you can simply tell them you would like to give them more information. Ask if they would be interested in a follow-up meeting, and arrange a suitable date and time.

CONSIDER THESE QUESTIONS FOR YOUR BUSINESS

- ✓ What events can you facilitate or host for potential customers?
- ✓ Should your events be online, offline or blended?
- ✓ Where do relevant events take place in your local area?
- ✓ Can you offer to speak at industry events?
- ✓ What kind of business network do you want to cultivate?
- ✓ Who exactly should you be adding to your network?
- ✓ How can you give a compelling sales pitch in two minutes or less?

BUSINESS COMMUNITIES

There are many **LOCAL BUSINESS COMMUNITIES** and Networks to connect with and assist you with your business. Suppose you feel a bit lost and don't know where to start. In that case, you can look at the following: Local Enterprise Offices, Small Firms Association, Networking Groups like Network Ireland, Skillnet, Regional LEADERs, Chambers of Commerce, Regional Skills and many other organisations. The people you know are the people who know and trust you already. Familiarity will help in the networking process as people are more likely to trust someone they know, so why not ask for help and get plugged into this valuable resource.

CONSIDER THESE QUESTIONS FOR YOUR BUSINESS

- ✓ What communities would benefit your business?
- ✓ Who are they, and how do you connect to them?
- ✓ How can you add value to the members of these communities?

Networking is vital; advertisements or traditional marketing can't compare to face-to-face communications. You may naturally pull back from networking when your business gets busy, as you won't have the time. It's of utmost importance that you make networking a priority. Delegate tasks to members of your team, which will give you time to make yourself available for networking.

AWARDS

Applying for awards and attending award ceremonies is a great way to get yourself recognised and generate interest in your product. The awards process is a brilliant way to boost employees' morale, build brand awareness and get free advertising for your company. Find out what awards are in your industry (your local Chamber of Commerce is a great place to start). Discover what the process is to get involved. Look at who has won previously. Why did they win? What made them stand out? And get your company involved in the next awards process. Being an award winner can be added as one of your unique selling points!

There are many different personality types and communication preferences, and not everyone enjoys interacting or socialising with others, so attending award ceremonies may be the last thing on your list. Certain personality types can experience social awkwardness leaving them feeling like they don't know how to fit in or know what to say to someone they don't already know.

If that sounds familiar, it is advisable to identify your skillset (strengths and areas for development) as early as possible. As a business owner, if you have a quiet personality and prefer to be in the background, even though you are brilliant at what you do but do not necessarily like the limelight, then identify this early and hire someone to represent you. Being shy or timid in business is perfectly acceptable – strengths come in many shapes and sizes. However, to get your product out to market, you must ensure you have someone to do the networking or customer-facing work on your behalf.

Another big challenge for many business owners is finding the time to network and attend these networking events and business awards. It is a shame not to make the most of them because they can become a valuable sales and marketing channel, highly effective in getting your product and company name out there.

For the extrovert who loves the limelight, the challenge can be the opposite, not putting enough effort into creating new products and keeping up with the day-to-day running of the business because they tend to spend too much time networking and attending events lose sight of why they are there. This example is extreme but not unheard of!

It's vital to get the balance right and hire for your business's interest to ensure that no area of your business gets neglected.

CONSIDER THESE QUESTIONS FOR YOUR BUSINESS

- ✓ What awards can you apply for that would elevate your brand?
- ✓ What is your personality type?
- ✓ What are your communication preferences?
- ✓ Do you enjoy networking, is your personality more introverted and would you prefer to outsource this?
- ✓ Who in your company is excellent at communicating?
- ✓ How much time have you allocated to networking?

SOCIAL MEDIA NETWORKING

Networking online allows you to connect with potential customers for free. It has never been easier for businesses to build relationships and gain exposure to a global market without ever having to leave their home. So it's a no-brainer to leverage the power of social media.

There are many social media platforms you can use for networking. LinkedIn is an obvious choice and particularly useful for Business to Business (B2B) connections. LinkedIn allows you to have a page to promote yourself as an individual and pages to promote your company, brand, products and services. You can reach your audience without leaving home by sharing posts, and articles, writing blogs, and vlogs. Linkedin also contains many diverse and interesting business groups. Take some time to see what groups would be helpful for you to join, then connect and follow these groups. The best way to connect with others in specific groups is to become an active participant by commenting on other people's posts, asking questions and showing genuine interest.

You can create company profiles on many other platforms if Linkedin doesn't fit what you want to achieve – for example, Twitter, Facebook, Instagram, YouTube, Snapchat, TikTok etc. Whatever platform you use, make sure it's somewhere your customers hang out and then connect with as many of them as possible and start conversations.

Be as interested in them and what they do; as you want them to be in you. Add value through your posts. Be informative, share what you know, and be helpful; your customers will gravitate to you.

You are an expert in your industry, and your followers will want to learn from you. Tell them about your company: how you got started, how you can help them, how your product is different, and so on.

"Tell, don't sell" is an excellent motto regarding your online presence. Tell your story, the benefits you can bring to potential customers and what problems you solve. I cannot stress this enough.

You can write personal messages online and comment on what other people discuss. Talk with them, get to know them, and find out about the things that matter to them most. You can like their posts, share their comments, and include them when you want to make decisions by asking for feedback and opinions.

COMMUNICATION

Communication is critical to the success of any business. It allows businesses to coordinate their activities, exchange information and ideas, and build relationships with customers, suppliers, partners, and employees. Good communication can help companies to run more efficiently and effectively, while poor communication can lead to misunderstanding, conflict, and inefficiency.

Every customer interaction is an opportunity for you and your business to shine. Clear and effective communication is essential to maintaining a good relationship with your customers, whether you're communicating via email, phone, in person, or social media. If they can't understand what you're saying, or if they feel like you're not listening to them, they're unlikely to stick around for long.

Even when there's a problem, excellent communication with your customer service team can go a long way to building lasting customer relationships. Your past and current customers gladly become advocates for your business or brand.

Many cost-effective communication tools are available that can enhance and automate customer communication. Let us focus on email marketing; Mailchimp is a free and straightforward tool to set up and manage your customer email list. You can build your customer base and target, track and analyse your emails. This tracking gives precious insights into the content your customers prefer to consume and what, on the other hand, does not resonate.

Tools like Mailchimp, Converkit and Unbounce also allow for effective personalisation of your customer communication which can be invaluable if you have different customer segments and a diverse product portfolio. The more a customer feels like you are talking just to them about what is most important to them, the higher the likelihood they will want to buy from you.

But even with all these wonderful platforms available, relationships always revert to customers' human interaction with your business. These are often the most memorable and can be a massive differentiation point for your business when you do them well. We have all experienced poor communication with a company – it causes frustration, disappointment and bad word of mouth (both on and offline). It can be costly for businesses to get this wrong.

Ensure your customer-facing employees are hired for their communication skills and trained in the latest customer experience service techniques. This investment will be money well spent, I promise you and will continue to pay dividends in the long term.

CONSIDER THESE QUESTIONS FOR YOUR BUSINESS

- ✓ Do you have a strategy around external communication?
- ✓ How do your customers currently rate your online and face-to-face communication?
- ✓ Has your customer-facing staff received adequate training to deliver excellent service?
- ✓ Are you leveraging available communication tools and software to elevate your brand?
- ✓ What content are your customers most interested in?

CONCLUSION

Great companies focus on their customers and their customer's requirements. Customers are people like you and me. If you treat them with respect, they will respond in kind. Ask them what they want, if they're satisfied and what you can do differently to better meet their needs.

You can have fantastic products, but your business may not be perceived positively unless you are a friendly, likeable person/brand.

Networking can help you shine a very positive light on your business and you as a person. Connections may not be immediate but will develop and convert over time. The goal is to connect and build meaningful relationships that last.

The common and mistaken assumption is that marketing is expensive, but it doesn't have to be. Some approaches and platforms are highly cost effective and can be easily implemented to meet your business needs. Always keep in mind how effective word of mouth can be.

Look at the Customer Journey and how it may be improved by looking after your current customer and enhancing their customer service and the products you offer them. They will become brand ambassadors and loyal advocates for your business. Remember the value you bring to your customer, don't be afraid to ask for referrals and focus on continuously adding value.

"The single greatest people skill is a highly developed and authentic interest in the other person".

Bob Burg

CUSTOMERS HEALTHCHECK

1. Have I segmented my customer base?
2. What is my sales strategy?
3. How am I advertising and promoting my business?
4. What channels do my customers use to buy my products and services?
5. How actively am I and my team in networking?
6. Could I consider entering an awards competition for my industry?
7. What social media channels am I present on?
8. Am I clear on how I want my brand represented online?
9. Have I considered using influencers to promote my brand?
10. What are my customers currently saying about my product or service?

NOTES

4: EMPLOYEES

"It doesn't make sense to hire smart people and tell them what to do; we hire smart people so they can tell us what to do".

Steve Jobs

In this chapter, you will find answers to the following questions:

- Why is the onboarding process necessary?
- Why should you always check references?
- Why do you need to keep personnel records and time/wage records?
- Why is new hire training required?
- How to ensure that employees comply with local regulations?
- Why do background checks, particularly for staff assigned financial duties?
- Why are employee Health and Safety awareness essential for staff and customers?

Figure 10: *Sub-Building Blocks for Employees*

Any business is only as good as its employees. That's why it's so important to get the right people on board and to set them up for success. In this chapter, we'll discuss how to find and hire the best employees, onboard them effectively, create a positive and productive workplace culture, manage performance, and invest in employee training and development. We'll also talk about succession planning and employee well-being. By the end of this chapter, you'll have a solid understanding of how to build a strong team that will help your business succeed.

Knowing where to start with the plethora of books and information about recruitment, team-building, performance management, and leadership can be overwhelming. So, in this chapter, I will concentrate on the key elements or essential points to note regarding:

- Recruitment
- Employee engagement
- Communications
- Team-building, and
- Compliance

RECRUITMENT

Recruitment is one of the most critical building blocks for any business. To succeed, having the right people on your team is essential. The wrong person in the wrong role can cost a company and cause many problems. That's why it's so important to take the time to find the right people for the job. With the right team in place, anything is possible!

Critical components of an effective recruitment strategy are:

1. Knowing what you need

The first step is to know what kind of person you need for the job. What skills and experience are required? What personality traits would be a good fit for your company culture? Once you know what you're looking for, you can narrow down your candidates.

2. Advertising the right way

The next step is ensuring you're advertising the role in the right places. Where will you find people with the skills and experience you're looking for? If you're not sure, ask around or do some research online.

3. Screening candidates properly

It's important to screen candidates carefully to ensure they're a good fit for the job. This screening includes interviewing them, checking references, and doing background checks.

4. Making the right offer

Once you've found the right person for the job, you must make them an offer they can't refuse. This offer means offering competitive salaries and benefits and clarifying your company's culture and what you expect from employees.

If you can get recruitment right, it will make a massive difference to the success of your business. So take the time to do it correctly!

It's also important to remember that whomever you hire for your business is a good fit for your business values. You want to hire people who understand your goals and are excited to help you achieve them. Someone may have all the skills and experience in the world but may cause you many headaches down the line if their values are very different to yours.

The best advice I can give you here is to recruit for values fit first and experience second. You can always provide training to address any skills gaps later.

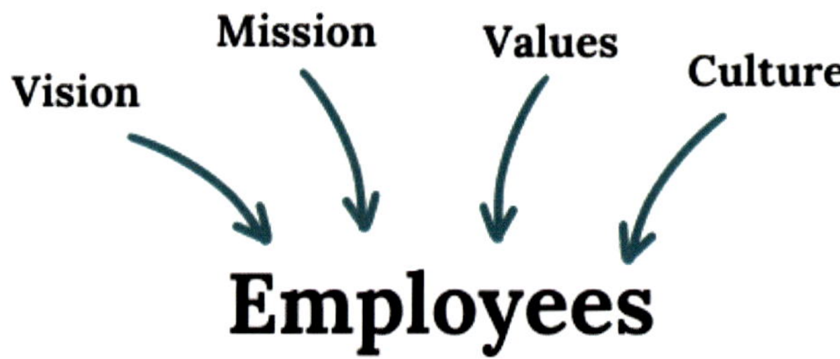

Figure 11: *Employees Must Align to your Company Culture*

ONBOARDING

Employee onboarding involves acclimatising new employees to their job and company culture. It is essential because it helps new employees feel comfortable in their new role, reduces turnover, and increases productivity. When done correctly, employee onboarding sets new hires up for success by providing them with the tools they need to be successful in their new role. By taking the time to onboard new employees properly, you can create a strong foundation for your business.

When you don't have an onboarding program, it can lead to several problems. New employees may feel lost and confused, leading to frustration and feeling overwhelmed. The overwhelm can lead to a higher turnover rate and decreased productivity. Additionally, without an onboarding program, you miss the opportunity to make an excellent first impression with your new hires.

Include many different elements in an employee onboarding program. First, you will have a plan for orienting new hires to their job duties. The onboarding might consist of providing job descriptions, explaining company policies, and giving them a tour of their work area. Next, you'll want to introduce them to co-workers and help them acclimate to the company culture. Finally, you should provide new employees with the resources they need to succeed in their roles. Some resources might include training materials, access to company manuals, and contact information for key personnel.

Too often, new employees are thrown in at the deep end and left to sink or swim. This lack of connection is terrible for morale and can lead to a high and costly turnover rate as employees feel unvalued or supported. A good employee onboarding program will help new employees transition into their roles smoothly and efficiently. By taking the time to invest in your employees from the very beginning, you create a robust and loyal workforce that will help your business thrive.

CULTURE

A company's culture is the personality of the organisation. It's what makes the company unique and sets it apart from others in its industry. A strong company culture can help attract and retain employees, customers, and clients. It can also help to improve communication and collaboration within the company. The company can be more successful when everyone is on the same page and working towards the same goal.

Culture is influential because it can help to create a sense of community within the company. It can also help to improve employee morale and motivation. A positive company culture can lead to increased productivity and profitability.

You must cultivate and nurture a solid company culture because it does not happen accidentally. The leaders of the company must set the tone and lead by example. They must also create policies and procedures that support the desired culture.

For your company to succeed, you need to have a strong foundation. That foundation is your company culture.

If you haven't put much thought into your own company's culture at this point - don't worry. You are not alone. Here are a few practical suggestions to lay culturally solid foundations:

1. Define your company's core values. These guiding principles will shape everything from your hiring decisions to how you handle customer complaints.
2. Communicate your company's culture to everyone who comes into contact with it. This communication includes employees, customers, vendors, and anyone else who might interact with your business.
3. Live your company's culture every day. The best way to do this is to model the behaviour you want to see in your employees. Your team will likely follow suit if you are respectful, honest, and hardworking.
4. Be consistent with your messaging. Your company culture should be evident in everything you do, from answering the phone to designing your marketing materials.
5. Reward employees who exemplify your company's culture. This reward could be in the form of bonuses, public recognition, or simply a handwritten note of thanks.
6. Encourage feedback and open communication. If something isn't working, don't be afraid to make changes. The goal is to create a company culture where everyone can be proud and feel heard.

Developing a strong company culture is essential for any business that wants to be successful. By taking the time to define your core values and communicate them to everyone who interacts with your business, you will be well on your way to creating a thriving organization.

CONSIDER THESE QUESTIONS FOR YOUR BUSINESS

- ✓ What are your business values and mission, and do they align with the employee's personal beliefs and values?
- ✓ Have you defined a company culture?
- ✓ Have you asked employees what we could do differently regarding their onboarding process?
- ✓ How do you know if a recruit is a great culture fit for your business?
- ✓ Do you have an onboarding program to ensure new hires have a smooth introduction to your company?

EMPLOYEE ENGAGEMENT

Employee Engagement is the level of commitment and involvement an employee has with their work and company. It is critical for any business because it ensures that employees are motivated and invested in their work. When employees are engaged, they are more productive, creative, and efficient. Additionally, engaged employees tend to stick around longer, which saves the company money in turnover costs. Engaged employees are also more likely to provide excellent customer service, which leads to repeat business and positive word-of-mouth. Simply put, employee engagement is essential for a company's bottom line. When employees are engaged, the whole company benefits.

How do you know if your employees are engaged? One way is to ask them directly. Conducting regular surveys is a great way to gauge employee engagement levels. Another way to tell is by observing employee behaviour. Do they seem excited and enthusiastic about their work? Are they willing to go the extra mile? If so, chances are they're engaged.

You can also look at companywide metrics such as productivity, customer satisfaction, and profitability. When these are up, it's a good indication that employees are engaged.

If you are concerned about your businesses employee engagement levels, you can do the following:

- Encourage more open communication between management and employees.
- Ensure employees feel like they are part of the team and their voices are heard.
- Offer opportunities for employee growth and development.

- Foster a positive work environment where employees feel appreciated.

There are some common misconceptions about what makes employees happy and engaged at work. Many believe that employees only care about money, but this is not always the case. Compensation is necessary, but it's not the only thing that matters. Employees also want to feel like they are doing meaningful work and that their contributions are valued. They want to be part of a team and have a chance to grow and develop their skills. Creating a positive work environment and culture is also key to engagement. When employees feel like they are part of something and making a difference, they are more likely to be engaged.

CONSIDER THESE QUESTIONS FOR YOUR BUSINESS

✓ What are the current levels of employee engagement in your business?

✓ How often do you ask your employees for feedback?

✓ What are the most common complaints from employees?

✓ What are your employee turnover and retention rates?

✓ Do you have an Employee Engagement strategy in place?

✓ What are the top 3 factors that drive employee engagement in your business?

✓ Is the compensation and benefits package you offer your employees competitive?

✓ How can you use your employee engagement strategy as a unique selling point from an employer brand perspective?

✓ Would your current and former employees recommend your business as a great place to work?

PERFORMANCE MANAGEMENT

Performance management is a process that helps businesses ensure that their employees are meeting or exceeding expectations. It involves setting goals, providing feedback, and measuring progress. A well-designed performance management system can help businesses improve employee productivity, identify training and development needs, and make better decisions about pay and promotions. It can also help employees feel more engaged in their work and motivated to achieve their goals.

PERSONAL DEVELOPMENT REVIEW (PDR): refers to a yearly review between the Manager and Employee. A PDR motivates employees and ensures they benefit from their hard work and commitment to the company. It is a valuable opportunity to reflect on their performance, potential, and development needs.

The Performance Management Process is an ongoing cycle that should be reviewed and updated regularly. By following these steps, you can create a system to help your business improve employee productivity and achieve its goals.

Let's go through each of the critical aspects of an effective Performance Management Strategy:

Set Clear and SMART Goals

The first step is to set clear and specific goals for employees. These goals should be aligned with the company's overall strategy. They should also be specific, achievable, measurable, relevant, and time-bound (SMART). Without clear goals, measuring employees' progress and determining whether they are meeting or exceeding expectations will not be easy to measure or track.

Conduct Regular Performance Discussions

Performance discussions should be held regularly, such as monthly or quarterly. These meetings allow managers to give employees feedback on their progress and help them identify areas for improvement. Conduct performance discussions constructively and positively, focusing on assisting them in improving their performance.

Provide Clear and Constructive Feedback

Feedback is a crucial part of the performance management process. It helps employees understand what they are doing well and where they need to improve. Feedback should be clear, concise, and specific. It should also be timely, objective, and delivered in a manner that promotes learning and growth.

Track Progress and Celebrate Successes

It's vital to track employees' progress over time to see how they are improving (or not). This data can identify trends and inform decisions about pay, promotions, and other recognition. Celebrating successes is also an essential part of performance management. When employees feel recognized and appreciated for their hard work, they are more likely to be motivated to maintain or improve their performance.

CONSIDER THESE QUESTIONS FOR YOUR BUSINESS

- ✓ Do your employees have clear goals, and do they understand how their performance is measured?
- ✓ Are you reviewing employees' performance regularly?
- ✓ Is positive and constructive feedback given?
- ✓ What do your employees think of the performance management process?
- ✓ Are performance issues addressed and rectified quickly?

LEARNING AND DEVELOPMENT

LEARNING and DEVELOPMENT (L&D) are critical for any business that wants to succeed. By providing employee training and development opportunities, businesses can ensure they have the skills and knowledge to achieve their goals. This training benefits the company and employees who can grow and develop within their roles.

Training is a vital part of L&D and is essential for businesses to provide employees with the opportunity to learn new skills and improve their performance. By investing in training, businesses can see a return in the form of increased productivity, higher quality work, and improved employee retention.

So if you're looking to invest in your business's future, Learning and Development is a great place to start. And don't forget, training doesn't just have to be for new employees - it can also be a valuable way to keep your existing team up-to-date on changes in the industry or company.

A great way to quickly determine what training your employees may need is to conduct a **TRAINING NEEDS ANALYSIS (TNA).** The TNA can help you identify gaps in your employees' skills so you can focus your training efforts where needed.

A comprehensive Training Needs Analysis would include the following:

- A review of your business's goals and objectives
- An analysis of your employee's current skills and knowledge
- An evaluation of your employees' training needs based on their roles within the company
- A plan for how to address any identified training needs

If you're unsure where to start with a Training Needs Analysis, many resources are available online, or you can speak to a Learning and Development professional. Once you understand your employees' training needs, you can develop a plan to best meet those needs.

There are many different formats of training on offer, but some standard options include the following:

- Classroom-based training: This type of training takes place in a traditional classroom setting and can be used to teach employees new skills or knowledge.
- Online training: Online training is a flexible option that employees can access anytime. Most training can be delivered online, from technical skills training to soft skills development.
- On-the-job training: This type of training involves employees learning new skills while they are working. It can be an effective way to provide employees with the hands-on experience they need to be successful in their roles.

No matter what type of training you decide to provide, it's essential to ensure that it is well-designed and delivered in a way that meets the needs of your employees. In other words, don't just throw a bunch of information at your employees and expect them to learn everything perfectly! Learning and Development is a necessary process that takes time and effort to get right, but it's worth it when you see the positive impact it has on your business.

CONSIDER THESE QUESTIONS FOR YOUR BUSINESS

✓ What skills are required to allow employees to carry out their roles effectively?

✓ What skills are required to develop employees to the next level of your organisation?

✓ Do you carry out TNA and employee competency evaluations?

✓ What future skills may your employees need to ensure your business remains relevant and competitive?

✓ How will the training be delivered and by whom?

✓ Can the training be carried out in-house, or should you hire a specialist to do the training?

✓ Have you identified statutory and mandatory training requirements?

PAYROLL

Payroll is the process of managing employee wages and compensation. It is an integral part of any business, ensuring that employees are paid accurately and on time. Payroll also helps to track employee hours worked, vacation days taken, and sick days used. This information is vital for budgeting and forecasting purposes. Without a sound payroll system, businesses can struggle to stay organized and may even face legal penalties for not properly paying their employees. Standard best practices when it comes to payroll management are:

- Establishing and maintaining clear communication channels between employees and payroll staff
- Keeping accurate records of employee hours worked, vacation days taken, and sick days used
- Making sure that all employees are paid accurately and on time
- Reviewing payroll reports regularly to look for errors or discrepancies
- Addressing any issues or concerns that arise in a timely and efficient manner.

It Is a statutory requirement to deduct income taxes from the payroll. In Ireland, the income taxes are **Pay As You Earn (PAYE)/ Pay Related Social Insurance (PRSI)/ Universal Social Charge (USC)** for employees. An employer must take care of the income tax obligations of its employee. The tax due is calculated according to the tax bracket in which the employee finds him or herself and is deducted from the total income before payment to the employee.

By following the above best practices, businesses can ensure that their payroll system runs smoothly and efficiently. This best practice, in turn, will help improve employee morale and motivation and reduce turnover rates. In addition, it will also save the business money in the long run by avoiding costly mistakes and penalties.

SUCCESSION

Succession planning is identifying and developing future leaders for your business. It's essential to have a succession plan in place because it ensures that your business will have the talent it needs to continue growing and thriving in the future. Without a succession plan, your business could be at risk if key employees leave or retire.

When you have a succession management program for your business, you can be confident that employees are identified and trained to take on leadership roles when the time comes. The succession plan can give you peace of mind as a business owner, knowing that your business will be in good hands even if you're no longer there to lead it.

There are many different ways to create a succession plan, but some key elements include identifying high-potential employees, providing training and development opportunities, and creating a clear path for advancement. By taking the time to develop a well-thought-out succession plan, you can ensure that your business will be able to survive and thrive for years to come.

RETENTION

Employee retention is the process of keeping employees happy and engaged with their work. It's important because it helps businesses keep good employees, reduces turnover, and saves money. There are many ways to improve employee retention, including offering competitive pay and benefits, providing training and development opportunities, and creating a positive work environment. Businesses can create a more stable and productive workforce by focusing on employee retention.

You may have read in the news recently about the "Great Resignation" of employees, particularly prevalent since the COVID-19 pandemic when an employee leaves their job, not because they were unhappy with it but because they saw an opportunity for a better work-life balance elsewhere. Resignation can be a big problem for businesses, leading to a high turnover rate and a loss of skilled employees.

"Experts suggest that two factors are fuelling this trend. While the pandemic served as the trigger, the seeds of the Great Resignation were sown well before – and until the deep-rooted factors causing workers to quit are addressed, resignations are unlikely to subside. People are also now looking at work and the role they want it to play in their lives differently and switching to jobs that better align with their new values. And, say the experts, the extent to which the looming slowdown will affect these quit rates remains to be seen." ***Source: BBC.com***

There are many things that businesses can do to improve employee retention and reduce the risk of the Great Resignation.

One way is to offer competitive pay and benefits. This package includes salary, bonuses, healthcare, and retirement savings plans. A competitive package can show your employees you value their skills and experience.

Another way to improve employee retention is to provide training and development opportunities. This training can help employees feel like they are progressing in their careers and have a chance to grow within the company. It can also make them more likely to stay with the company long-term.

Finally, businesses can create a positive work environment. Some examples include flexible work hours, working-from-home options, and a supportive culture. Creating a positive environment can make employees happy and engaged, leading to lower turnover and a more productive workforce.

Employee retention is an essential issue for businesses to consider. Businesses can improve employee retention by offering competitive pay and benefits, providing training and development opportunities, and creating a positive work environment.

CONSIDER THESE QUESTIONS FOR YOUR BUSINESS

- ✓ What jobs are critical roles for your business?
- ✓ Who carries out these roles, and are the succession plans in place?
- ✓ What would happen if this person left in the morning?
- ✓ How would this affect the company?
- ✓ Are there sub-contractors that can do this job?
- ✓ Is everything being done to ensure employees are engaged and likely to stay with the company?

WELLBEING

Workplace wellness is the promotion of healthier lifestyle choices in the workplace. Employees who are physically and mentally fit have a positive outlook on life and are more productive, absent less often and cost their employers less health care expenses. A wellness program can also improve morale and reduce stress levels among employees.

Well-being in the workplace is important for many reasons. First, it helps to create a healthy and productive work environment. Secondly, it can help to improve employee morale and motivation. Finally, it can also lead to increased profits for businesses. All these factors make workplace well-being a subject worth looking at.

There are many different components to workplace wellness, but some of the most important include the following:

- Healthy eating
- Regular exercise
- Stress management, and
- Getting enough sleep.

As more companies streamline their workforces and require their employees to do more with less and an increased focus on mental health and wellbeing, the importance of workplace wellness programs has never been greater.

If you are interested in creating a workplace wellness program for your business, there are a few things to keep in mind.

- First, you need to identify the needs of your employees and what would work best for them.
- Secondly, you must ensure that your program is sustainable and that you have the resources to support it.
- Finally, you must promote your program and ensure that employees know about and participate.

Workplace wellness is a growing trend in businesses today, and for good reason. It's important for both employers and employees to be healthy and happy at work. By promoting well-being in the workplace, you can create a healthier and more productive work environment for everyone.

CONSIDER THESE QUESTIONS FOR YOUR BUSINESS

- ✓ Are employees demotivated or showing signs of stress?
- ✓ What is the work/life balance like in your organisation?
- ✓ Do you have a wellness program, and are your employees actively participating in it?
- ✓ Do your employees have concerns or require well-being-related assistance?
- ✓ Are you actively talking about well-being in the workplace?

CONCLUSION

Employees are a company's most important asset. Your employees are the ones who work day in and day out to make your business successful. They deserve your respect and appreciation. But more than that, they need to feel like they're part of a team working together towards a common goal. When employees feel valued and supported, they are more likely to be productive and happy in their work.

Don't be afraid to have open and honest conversations about your employee's experience working in your business. Every organisation has room for improvement! Seek feedback and take action where you can. Your time and effort will pay dividends.

"Employees are offering us an essential part of their life. If we don't use their time effectively, we are wasting their lives".

Eiji Toyoda, Former President & Chairman of Toyota Motor Corporation

---

EMPLOYEES HEALTHCHECK

1. What is the culture of my company? And can I describe it?

2. What are my values and goals, and whom do I want to recruit to live up to them?

3. What is the skillset most required right now by my business? What Skills, Knowledge and Attributes (SKA) are required to carry out the role?

4. When is the right time to hire the next person? How will this person add value to my company? Can I teach or mentor this employee? What will happen if I do hire or don't hire? Have I thought this through? Do I need a body in that position?

5. Can I trust that my employees will work on their own initiative? How much time will they require from me?

6. Do I have regular team meetings or board meetings? Are minutes of meetings documented, with actions and timelines?

7. Are all employees trained for their roles, and how can I assess them? Do I have a set of Key Performance Indicators (KPIs) for all key staff?

8. Are all staff committed to improvement? How do I know?

9. Do I empower and encourage my team on Continuous Improvement and new ideas? Are good ideas rewarded?

10. Do all staff get regular personal development reviews and align operational goals with the strategic objectives?

NOTES

5: CASHFLOW

"Revenue is Vanity; Profit is Sanity; Cash is King."

Unknown

In this chapter, you will find answers to the following questions:

- Why exactly is Cash King?
- Why is it critical to have quick access to cash?
- Why are reputation and credit references essential?
- Why meaningful customer and supplier relationships are important?
- How do you correctly complete a Cashflow?
- Why is it crucial to think about unplanned events and have a contingency plan?

Figure 12: *Sub-Building Blocks for Cashflow*

Cash flow is the lifeblood of any business. Cashflow is the money that comes in and out of business. Without positive cash flow, a business will quickly run into trouble. That's why it is essential to understand the basics of cash flow and how to manage it effectively.

Many larger corporates have cash-pooling, where bank accounts are linked to the head office, and transfers are requested when cash is required. They don't need to think about cash flow daily; money will always be available to meet their demands. But this may be a challenge if you are a smaller company and don't have easy access to cash. You must know your cash balance at all times. Far too many companies are closed down because they cannot pay the bank or lose good employees and suppliers as they cannot pay them on time. These closures can be easily avoided with better cash management processes and access to appropriate data.

In the next chapter, I speak about implementing simple accounting packages to track all invoicing and business transactions; this gives you better visibility of your cash position. The key to running a successful business, emerging from any crisis or allowing for scalability, is your company's ability to generate positive **FREE CASH FLOW**. We will look at this later in the chapter.

Any unforeseen event or rapid growth can negatively impact your business and be very demanding on cash flow. Having a solid **BALANCE SHEET** (discussed in chapter 6) will help you weather the storm as you can divert the lack of **CASH INFLOW** with greater access to capital and cash reserves.

Take, for example, the scenario where you don't have access to cash or the internal resources required to cover your **CASH OUTFLOW**. This lack of access to money is one of the biggest challenges you will face as a small business!

Your sales and cash will be affected if there is a significant decline in your products' consumption. Cash-in-hand will rapidly deteriorate, with sales receipts reduced, fixed expenses such as employee costs, rent, and utilities must be paid regardless of revenue, and suppliers are still due for payment. If your business fails to navigate the unwanted issue of negative free cash flow, insolvency or permanent closure may soon be on the horizon.

As a business owner, you want to manage net cash flow to respond and be ready for any eventuality. It is essential to take a sensible approach to maintain stakeholder relationships and keep the lines of communication open. You cannot merely avoid paying **CREDITORS,** or your goodwill and reputation will rapidly erode.

AVAILABLE CASH

An essential topic in business is to generate profit, but when you strip away the costs of marketing, management and product development, the purpose is to be profitable, make a difference with your product or service, and ultimately generate cash. You need money to make money. There will be costs in developing and providing your products and services before any sale occurs, right?

CONSIDER THESE QUESTIONS FOR YOUR BUSINESS

- ✓ What is the primary source of your cash?
- ✓ What happens if you don't receive invoice payments on time?
- ✓ What standard credit terms do you offer customers?
- ✓ Do you regularly review and re-negotiate your payment terms with vendors and suppliers?
- ✓ Do you measure operational efficiency to see where you can improve the process?
- ✓ Do you manage your insurance policies and shop around? Similarly, with other expenses?
- ✓ Can you make money from by-products? Can you improve your product or get into a new niche market?
- ✓ How are the relationships with your stakeholders? Are you familiar with who they are?

Cash flow, therefore, needs to be one of your highest priorities. Cash flow refers to the net amount of money a business can use to make payments. Think of it as the cash available in your bank when you have forgotten your credit card. If you want to make a purchase, you use that cash. Unfortunately, this is an important aspect that is often overlooked in business. There is a difference between organically generated cash in your business and money temporarily borrowed or investments made into the business.

Many smaller companies mismanage their cash flow and do not make it past their first five years in business. Problems start when, for instance, stock needs to be ordered, but there is no money to pay for it. Great companies fail because suppliers have a 30-day payment policy, and the most significant client might have a 60-day payment policy.

These terms mean that if the business bought and sold stock in January, it only received payment in March. It had to pay its supplier's invoice in 30 days at the end of February, and during that time, the following order was already due. On top of that, your business has many other expenses and salaries to pay. Your business will have to close if you can't stay on top of your business-critical payments.

Generating cash flow is necessary and takes a lot of care and management. This cash should be generated from your company's work and should be the priority of a healthy company that funds itself and has the culture and the discipline to remain vigilant on its finances. External funding is temporary and should not be targeted as the first option.

CASHFLOW

You can improve cash flow management by adopting a structure that helps identify your cash flow drivers and engage **STAKEHOLDERS.**

Some essential planning tips are listed below:

- Complete cash projections on a daily, weekly, or monthly basis;
- Analyse **WORKING CAPITAL,** the cash flow between purchasing stock, receivables (debtors) and payables (creditors);
- Delay any **CAPITAL EXPENDITURE** (fixed asset) projects;
- Review all banking facilities, e.g., interest rates and personal bank guarantees;
- Identify which payments are unnecessary or can be reduced or eliminated – for example, rent, marketing spend, office supplies etc.
- Increase creditor days and reduce debtor days; arrange to pay your suppliers as late as possible and agree on upfront payments with your customers or discounts if paid early.
- Analyse current spending and compare supplier prices;
- Look at outstanding invoices. Are there any bad debts to be written off? How can you negotiate these?
- Assess available external funding supports;
- Engage early with all stakeholders and be transparent; Key relationships are essential with Customers, Employees, Suppliers and Investors;
- Engage with landlords to arrange a rent reduction or rent freeze;
- Engage with banks to agree on loan moratoriums or payment breaks;

- Keep up-to-date on customer invoicing and consistently follow up on receipts;
- Deliver on negotiated agreements between your business and all stakeholders;
- Optimise the cash outflows of the company;
- Investigate all direct debits. Are any out-of-date or non-essential;
- Update your **BUDGET** and **FORECAST** to highlight the current situation; or Create a **BUSINESS PLAN** to outline the strength of the business case outside of any crisis; (more in Chapter 7)
- Complete regular variance analysis between actual financial results *versus* budget/forecast; this will help with decision-making and maybe pivot the business early if noticeable variances arise.
- Adjust your action plan according to current circumstances. Undertake scenario (What-if?) analysis by changing values to see the difference in outcome;

UNFORESEEN EVENTS

Unforeseen events can destroy a business, look at the impact of the pandemic, but you can budget for such an event. You can always allocate funds towards unexpected events or the "what if scenario" in your budget. In your personal life, your car might break down, or your plumbing might leak. The same goes for businesses. The only difference is that unexpected events can be far more severe in business. E.g. **REPAIR AND MAINTENANCE (R&M);** Having to repair a delivery truck that breaks down might stop your delivery business from making money. The event does not need to be hugely significant but can have a considerable impact.

Communication is at the core of conducting any business successfully and having strong relationships with all stakeholders.

Communication can help in unforeseen circumstances, as stakeholders can be more patient when they have up-to-date Financial Information. This is important because all parties know what is happening and what is required of them through proper communication.

The CoVID-19 pandemic was utterly unforeseen but impacted hundreds of thousands of businesses internationally. Nobody could have ever known what was in store. Many small businesses did not have the extra cash or access to it, and no contingency plan was in place. This lack of money meant they had to lay employees off when the money stopped coming in and even closed their doors. The companies that survived were the ones that could continue working regardless of income and have cash in the bank to pivot their business.

Even losing a key client, you rely on for your cash flow can devastate a business. That's why you need to make sure to allocate enough funds for unforeseen events and know the impact your customers have on your business. Also, consider any risk associated with your critical suppliers, as you may need alternative suppliers in the event of closures.

CONSIDER THESE QUESTIONS FOR YOUR BUSINESS

- ✓ Do you know the impact your key customers have on your cash flow?
- ✓ Do you purchase unique products that are hard to get anywhere else?
- ✓ What happens if this supplier goes out of business?
- ✓ How familiar are you with your supply chain and its effect on your cash flow?
- ✓ Do you have a contingency plan?

CASHFLOW STATEMENT

You can set up a Cashflow statement forecast similar to the one below. Look at what receipts you have due in, what you must pay out, and your current bank balance. Having a detailed cash flow statement allows for better decision-making regarding priority payments.

You can be as detailed or as straightforward as you want with this **CASHFLOW STATEMENT** – for example, instead of supplier payments on one line, you can list all your expenses and analyse them by cost.

CASHFLOW TEMPLATE

Company Name

As at (Day-Month-Year)

Monthly / Weekly / Quarterly

	Opening Balance	Jan	Feb	Mar	Apr	May	Jun	Jul	Aug	Sep	Oct	Nov	Dec	Grand Total
Bank as at beginning of period (A)	(A)													
CASH INFLOWS														
Customer Receipts														
Other Receipts														
Transfers/Deposits In														
Total Cash InFlow per month (B)	(B)	€0	€0	€0	€0	€0	€0	€0	€0	€0	€0	€0	€0	€0
CASH OUTFLOWS														
Supplier Payments														
Other Payments														
Transfers/Deposits Out														
Total Cash Outflow (C)	(C)	€0	€0	€0	€0	€0	€0	€0	€0	€0	€0	€0	€0	€0
TOTAL NETFLOWS PER MONTH (D)	(D=B-C)	€0	€0	€0	€0	€0	€0	€0	€0	€0	€0	€0	€0	€0
CUMULATIVE BANK BALANCE (E)	(E=A+D)	€0	€0	€0	€0	€0	€0	€0	€0	€0	€0	€0	€0	
CLOSING BANK BALANCE (F)	€0													

Figure 13: *Sample Cashflow Statement*

CONCLUSION

When running a business, ensure you manage your business's cash flow and other financial aspects to the best of your ability. There is a significant demand on business owners' time, so it might be an option to work with part-time finance directors or experienced accountants to support you with this aspect of your business.

You don't want an opportunity to present itself only to find you can't pursue it due to a lack of cash or available funds. Millions of businesses have experienced issues with their cash flow. This lack of opportunity doesn't have to be the case for you. Manage your cash closely, and give your business a fighting chance!

"Never take your eyes off the cash flow because it is the lifeblood of your business."

Richard Branson

CASHFLOW HEALTHCHECK

1. Is cash something I look at regularly within my business?
2. Are bank reconciliations carried out regularly?
3. Is my company up to date on invoicing?
4. Do I know where I can access finance if I need it?
5. Do I have a savings account or money set aside for a rainy day?
6. Do I know how much cash I need to keep my business afloat?
7. Do I measure the impact my biggest customer has on my business?
8. Do I have access to alternative suppliers should the need arise, and what relationship do I have with them?
9. When did I last negotiate prices with suppliers?
10. What are the interest rates on my long-term loans? How much is outstanding, and what are the terms?

NOTES

6: ACCOUNTS

"Accounting is the language of business".

Warren Buffet

In this chapter, you will find answers to the following questions:

- Why do you require access to management accounts?
- Why do you need to know what makes up all balances on your Balance Sheet?
- Why should you understand the Profit & Loss Account?
- Is it easy to access up-to-date, accurate and complete account information?
- Do you have to file financial statements with the **CRO** – **COMPANIES REGISTERED OFFICES?**
- Why do you have to be audit-ready, and why are audits so important?

Figure 14: *Sub-Building Blocks for Accounts*

Understanding financial and non-financial data in your business is essential and helps ensure you make accurate and high-quality business decisions. It's also vital to continually integrate information from across the business to help achieve organisational **OBJECTIVES**. Most companies have a management accountant or financial controller at the heart of decision-making. They will "connect the dots" and recognise how the different parts of the business come together to create value. They will help business owners understand and tell the business story through the accounts, income, costs, risks and opportunities.

ACCOUNTING SYSTEMS

Some companies work from one end of the year to the other with no management accounts or data to know how their business is doing; all their decision-making is based on guesswork and the bank balance.

MANAGEMENT ACCOUNTS consist of the following:

1. Profit & Loss Account
2. Cashflow statement
3. Balance Sheet.

It's best not to circulate this set of confidential reports throughout the business.

There are many simple accounting packages, cloud or otherwise, to give you access to this information. Some popular examples are Xero, SAGE and SURF. Accounting packages can also integrate directly with your bank, and you can have invoices emailed via an AUTO-ENTRY System to your accounts package. This automation saves time by moving away from manual invoice entry and creates more accurate and consistent invoice postings.

You can also set up sales quotes on these accounts packages and convert them to invoices when approved. Monthly, you can have all entries up-to-date, the bank account(s) reconciled and then print off a Profit & Loss account (P&L) and a Balance Sheet. You will have access to dashboards for **AGED DEBTORS** (List of all Customer Invoices not yet received) and **AGED CREDITORS** (List of all Suppliers' Invoices not yet paid). These reports allow you to know who and what to follow up on and when. You can also set up email invoicing, email remittance advice, and automatic monthly statements from these accounting packages.

Imagine how less stressed you might feel by having this information at your fingertips and not on your to-do list. You don't have to think of everything; you can have it on a system – in fact, many cloud systems also offer access via a smartphone. These systems are more easily accessible than the cumbersome systems from once upon a time, allowing you much more time to put into other areas of your business.

Of course, you need someone who understands bookkeeping or accounts to run this system for you (or you could consider outsourcing it if you don't have someone in your business with this skill set).

CONSIDER THESE QUESTIONS FOR YOUR BUSINESS

- ✓ What information do you have in spreadsheets that you could collate into an accounting package?
- ✓ How long does it take to collate data when required?
- ✓ Do you have bank reconciliations up to date?
- ✓ Does someone manually post invoices? Can you automate this process?
- ✓ Are your financial management processes documented and kept up to date?
- ✓ Who has access to confidential financial information, and how is this kept secure?
- ✓ What is the most time-consuming aspect of your business's financial/accounting? Can these be simplified, automated, or outsourced?

PROFIT & LOSS

Many companies make the **PROFIT AND LOSS (P&L)** their go-to document. The P&L summarises the company's performance over a particular period. It can be looked at as frequently as the manager requires: monthly, quarterly, year-to-date (YTD), this financial year or customised to any period you wish to analyse. It looks at the revenue or sales for the period and any costs or expenses paid out in that same period.

Costs or expenses can be grouped into profit centres where possible so that each manager can have a budget and know their spending and how it compares at any given time. Analyse the P&L performance *versus* last year and budget, with any seasonality taken into account. See Chapter 7 for more information on Budgets.

If your company deals with foreign currency, this can be taken into consideration also. Suppose you deal with high volumes of foreign currency. In that case, **HEDGING** can be arranged with your bank so that you fix in your local currency equivalent and know your local currency value of the transaction when it comes to fruition.

TURNOVER

Turnover is also referred to as sales, income or gross revenue.

Sometimes revenue and turnover may be confused as they are so closely related. Revenue looks at what your business has generated through selling your product or services. It is the total value of your sales.

On the other hand, **TURNOVER** is the income generated through all economic activities by the company. If your company has investments and other income forms other than selling its primary product or service, this forms part of the turnover. It is also the starting point for calculating how much profit a company is making. Your turnover is the first point of reference to know how a business is doing and appears as the first figure on the profit and loss account.

For further analysis, turnover must be classified into products/services, categories, departments or cost centres. The more you break down your Revenue Streams, the more you can analyse and make targeted decisions about your business.

DIRECT COSTS

Your **DIRECT COSTS** are the cost related to producing goods for sale. These may be the raw materials, supplies, labour, and manufacturing overheads needed to make the product that the company will then sell

The same applies to services rendered. For example, if you are offering training to companies, the cost of advertisement, the fuel for your employee to get to the training location, and the employee's salary will all be part of the direct costs to your company.

GROSS MARGIN

GROSS MARGIN relates to the direct profit of the product. The difference in how much it costs you to make the product versus how much you get when you sell it.

Turnover/Sales Less Direct Costs = Gross Margin

Gross Margin Divided by Turnover/Sales = Gross Margin %

Gross Margin % relates to how much this margin is as a % of the sales. If, for instance, your margin is 20% of the total Sales. This figure is hugely important; if your business expenses or other overheads are more than 20% of sales, you will be in a loss situation. You might understand this more clearly on the sample Profit & Loss template below.

It would help if you understood the gross margin by product. Some products will be more profitable than others. So break it down and assign costs as much as possible to the right products.

OVERHEADS

OVERHEADS are also referred to as indirect costs and can be further classified into Fixed and Variable Costs. They are costs that a company incurs whether it is actively producing goods or not; they are primarily planned expenses. Rent paid every month, office workers' salaries, insurance and utilities are the most straightforward examples that come to mind.

Overheads or indirect costs can quickly affect the bottom line of a company. Many companies opt to rent a massive office space, whereas a smaller space would suffice. Both get the same job done, but the first company takes more from the profit at the end of the month. Look at the different overheads and see where you can make savings.

Keeping your overheads low is something that everyone hears about but may lose sight of. It pays to be prudent and only incur the necessary expenses for the company's growth.

CONSIDER THESE QUESTIONS FOR YOUR BUSINESS

- ✓ Do you analyse your sales by category?
- ✓ What revenue streams do you have?
- ✓ Do you know your margin by category or cost centre?
- ✓ How often do you analyse overheads?
- ✓ What is the % growth over the past years, and in what areas?
- ✓ How many employees do you have?
- ✓ What are Labour costs compared to sales?
- ✓ Do you have access to all the information you need?

Another important term is **OPERATING PROFIT,** also known as Net Profit. After taking account of all costs incurred to sell your goods or services and all overheads incurred to run your business, what profit or loss is left?

You may also have heard of **(EBIT) EARNINGS BEFORE INTEREST AND TAX,** the profit before accounting for any interest or taxes.

I look at variances in more detail in the Budget Chapter. **VARIANCES** are the difference between your actual costs and last year's values, your budget, or what you thought it would be. Having access to these variances will trigger questions for you. You will want to understand why did these differences happen? Is there anything that you could have done differently, or is there anything you can change now to improve the situation before things get worse?

Variances can be negative and positive. What are you doing right, and can you do more of that? So you can see why having access to this data monthly is essential in running your business. If you wait until the end of the year to get the financial statements from your accountant, you will have lost out on early decision-making or pivots that could have changed your business.

PROFIT AND LOSS TEMPLATE

Company Name

As at (Day-Month-Year)

Description	Prior Period	Budget	Actual Period	Prior Period % of Sales	Budget Period % of Sales	Actual Period % of Sales	Variance Actual V's Prior	Variance Actual V's Budget
SALES / REVENUE								
Product/Service 1				0.0%	0.0%	0.0%		
Product/Service 2				0.0%	0.0%	0.0%		
Product/Service 3				0.0%	0.0%	0.0%		
Total Sales Revenue [A]	**0**	**0**	**0**	**0.0%**	**0.0%**	**0.0%**	0	0
COST OF SALES								
Product/Service 1				0.0%	0.0%	0.0%		
Product/Service 2				0.0%	0.0%	0.0%		
Product/Service 3				0.0%	0.0%	0.0%		
Total Cost of Sales [B]	**0**	**0**	**0**	**0.0%**	**0.0%**	**0.0%**	0	0
Gross Profit/Margin [C=A-B]	**0**	**0**	**0**	**0.0%**	**0.0%**	**0.0%**	0	0
OVERHEADS / EXPENSES								
Advertising				0.0%	0.0%	0.0%		
Direct marketing				0.0%	0.0%	0.0%		
Health & Safety				0.0%	0.0%	0.0%		
Software licenses				0.0%	0.0%	0.0%		
Patents				0.0%	0.0%	0.0%		
Wages and salaries				0.0%	0.0%	0.0%		
Consultancy & Professional Fees				0.0%	0.0%	0.0%		
Supplies				0.0%	0.0%	0.0%		
Meals and entertainment				0.0%	0.0%	0.0%		
Rent or Rates				0.0%	0.0%	0.0%		
Telephone				0.0%	0.0%	0.0%		
Utilities				0.0%	0.0%	0.0%		
Depreciation				0.0%	0.0%	0.0%		
Insurance				0.0%	0.0%	0.0%		
Repairs and maintenance				0.0%	0.0%	0.0%		
Other expenses (specify)				**0.0%**	**0.0%**	**0.0%**		
Total Expenses [D]	**0**	**0**	**0**	**0.0%**	**0.0%**	**0.0%**	0	0
Income from Operations [E=C-D]	**0**	**0**	**0**	**0.0%**	**0.0%**	**0.0%**	0	0
Other Income [F]	**0**	**0**	**0**	**0.0%**	**0.0%**	**0.0%**	0	0
Taxes								
Corporation taxes				0.0%	0.0%	0.0%		
Total Taxes [G]	**0**	**0**	**0**	**0.0%**	**0.0%**	**0.0%**	0	0
Net Profit [H=E+F-G]	**0**	**0**	**0**	**0.0%**	**0.0%**	**0.0%**	0	0

Figure 15: *Sample Profit & Loss Account*

BALANCE SHEET

The Balance Sheet is an essential document in business. It reflects the balance of what you own in your business **(ASSETS)** *versus* what you owe from your company (**LIABILITIES**). A Balance Sheet gives you a financial picture of a specific point in time. It also includes what the owner or shareholder has contributed in the form of investment. As its name suggests, it has to balance, and the other documents it integrates into are the Profit & Loss account and Cashflow statement. If a posting is made incorrectly in the P&L, you may not notice it in the P&L, but you may see that the balances on the balance sheet don't add up. It's essential to be 100% comfortable agreeing with all balances in your Balance Sheet, so you can be satisfied that there is no duplication or anything hidden or accidentally written off in the P&L.

Ensure you agree with your Balance Sheet balances, what you own, what you owe, and how much you have contributed to the company. You want to own more than you owe and keep the balance sheet positive.

SHAREHOLDERS refers to anyone who has invested in the business and holds a portion of the share capital.

Companies prepare audited annual accounts, but many meet more regularly to affect change and the outcome of these accounts. Decisions are made throughout the year to affect the business.

CONSIDER THESE QUESTIONS FOR YOUR BUSINESS

- ✓ Do you have regular board meetings?
- ✓ Who looks for information from your business?
- ✓ Do you have a listing of the shareholders and how often they would like information on the business?

ASSETS

From an accounting perspective, assets are any resource the business owns that will add value. Having control over a resource also makes it an asset. The meaning of an asset is no different from personal belongings. Your house or car can be seen as an asset as you own them and use them to produce value.

The critical aspect to consider is that an asset produces positive economic value. This means a company's building rented out to another company is an asset since it creates positive economic value. However, that same building, left unoccupied with many levies and taxes, is now a liability (see below).

There are two classifications of Assets: **FIXED ASSETS,** also known as non-current assets. Fixed Assets are tangible, and you can touch/hold them for use in the business. They are not readily available for sale or not easily converted to cash, but you can sell or convert them if you no longer require them to run your business. **CURRENT ASSETS** convert quickly or easily into money. Examples are Stock, Debtors, Prepayments and Cash. Know the most recent value of your current assets.

AGED DEBTORS or ACCOUNTS RECEIVABLE refers to the amount of money you have yet to receive from customers for goods or services you deliver. Invoices you have given for work completed or products sold, but you have not yet received payment. Follow up on invoices regularly, and ensure they are managed closely to ensure payment.

Check also that the STOCK value reflects its actual value and that there is no obsolete stock to write off. How often do you perform a stocktake?

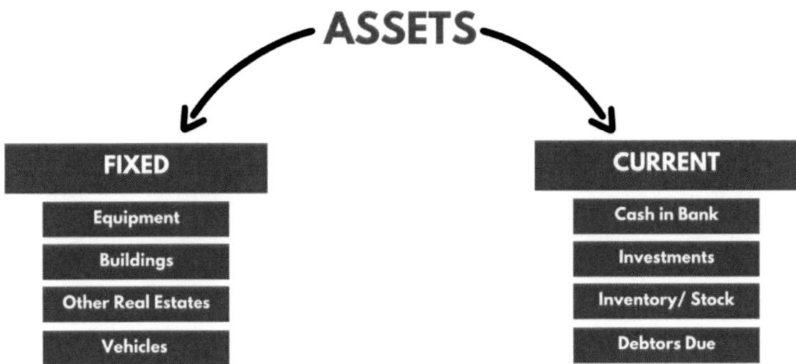

Figure 16: *Different Asset Types as seen in the Balance Sheet*

LIABILITIES

A liability is something a person or a company owes, broken into **SHORT-TERM** and **LONG-TERM LIABILITIES.** Long-Term Liabilities are due in more than one year, and repayment is expected soon for short-term liabilities. The perfect example is bank debt. You borrow money at a particular time and repay that debt later. This debt will then lessen the money you earn in future, as you will have to repay it plus interest.

An example of a short-term liability is an **OVERDRAFT.** An overdraft refers to a facility with your bank that, if you don't have enough cash and want to pay a bill, the amount will still go out of your bank account and allow your bank balance to go into a negative.

AGED CREDITORS / ACCOUNTS PAYABLE: the amount of money owed to suppliers for goods or services delivered to your business. Are all invoices up to date on your system? Do you have old invoices that you know are not due? Are there any duplicate invoices listed and already paid? Look at the aged listing regularly and ensure that you check invoices against supplier statements monthly.

Other liabilities include:

- Mortgage debt
- Any payable accounts
- Money owed to suppliers
- Wages owed to your employees
- Outstanding Taxes
- Bank debt

Liabilities are not necessarily always a bad thing. For example, borrowing to buy a car on credit to make more deliveries is not seen as bad credit because it grows your business. The above-mentioned empty building that keeps demanding repairs and payments is a liability.

The exact line between liability and asset can sometimes be confusing. Generally speaking, if something negatively impacts your future economic benefits or earnings, it is a liability, but loans are liabilities and can positively impact the business to help with investment and cash flow.

BALANCE SHEET TEMPLATE		
Company Name		
As at (Day-Month-Year)		
ASSETS		
Fixed Assets		
Property - Cost		0.00
Property - Accumulated Depreciation		0.00
Office equipment and IT - Cost		0.00
Office equipment and IT - Accumulated Depreciation		0.00
Fixtures and fittings - Cost		0.00
Fixtures and fittings - Accumulated Depreciation		0.00
Motor Vehicles - Cost		0.00
Motor Vehicles - Accumulated Depreciation		0.00
Total Fixed Assets (A)		**(A)**
Current Assets		
Stock	0.00	
Debtors	0.00	
Prepayments	0.00	
Bank - Current A/C	0.00	
Bank - Saving A/C	0.00	
Total Current Assets (B)	**(B)**	
TOTAL ASSETS (C)		**(C=A+B)**
LIABILITIES		
Current Liabilities		
Trade Creditors	0.00	
Accruals	0.00	
Bank Overdraft	0.00	
Directors Loan Accounts	0.00	
Payroll Taxes	0.00	
Corporation Tax Liability	0.00	
VAT Liability	0.00	
Total Current Liabilities (D)	**(D)**	
Net Current Assets (G)	**(G= B-D)**	
Long Term Liabilities		
Long Term Loan	0.00	
Total Long Term Liabilities (E)	**(E)**	
TOTAL LIABILITIES (F)		**(F=D+E)**
TOTAL NET ASSETS (H)		**(H=C-F)**
EQUITY		
Capital		0.00
Share Premium		0.00
Capital Redemption Reserve		0.00
Profit & Loss Prior Years		0.00
Net Profit / Loss (prior year(s))		0.00
Net Profit / Loss (current year)		0.00
Total Equity		**(I)**
Balance Check (I=H)		**(I=H=Zero)**

Figure 17: *Sample Balance Sheet Template*

CONSIDER THESE QUESTIONS FOR YOUR BUSINESS

- ✓ Do you have access to the Balance Sheet?
- ✓ How often do you do a stocktake?
- ✓ Are your Aged Debtors and Creditors up-to-date?
- ✓ Is there potential for Bad Debt?
- ✓ Do you know what makes up all balances on the balance sheet, and do you have a backup for the same?
- ✓ Is your bank reconciliation automated?
- ✓ How often do you converse about cash flow and interest rates with your bank?

BOARD MEETINGS

Most companies at the growth stage have regular board meetings. There is no hard and fast rule on how to perform or set up these board meetings. So for maximum benefit, arrange this with the **BOARD OF DIRECTORS** on what makes sense for your company. It's important to know what direction you want your company to go in, what you will cover in these meetings and go to the meeting well prepared. Prepare the agenda in advance and send it to the board before the meeting, allowing them sufficient time to review it.

Ensure someone takes minutes at these meetings and reports to the board with complete actions, the action owner and deadlines for each. You will want to review the previous board minutes before the following board meeting to ensure that the company moves forward.

Your CFO or finance contact is usually responsible for compiling the **BOARD PACK**. You will want this board pack to be prepared well before any meeting to ensure the information is correct and you have time to review it before its presented. Forward this to the board members in advance, as this information will guide the discussions and decision-making during the board meeting.

The board will discuss the company's strengths, human resources, forecasts, capital expenditure, and finances. **DASHBOARDS** are great for discussion and analysis, as the following chapter covers. However, the finance manager will usually be equipped with details on the reports and the data behind the figures and variables within the business.

It's great to have a one-page dashboard as a high-level summary to start, but other documents to include in the board pack are:

BOARD MEETING CHECKLIST
1. Copy of Profit and loss Statement - Actual V Prior Year & Budget
2. P&L Variances and explanations for each
3. % Growth over time
4. % Margins and explanations for any changes
5. Overhead Analysis
6. Departmental Analysis - % Margin for each
7. Labour Rate %
8. Copy of the Balance Sheet
9. Aged Debtors and Creditors Listing
10. Explanation for all balances listed in the Balance Sheet
11. Cashflow Statement
12. Bank Balances and Variances
13. Consolidation Reports if more than one company
14. Organisation Chart and any changes
15. Any other reports specific to the industry

AUDITS

Audits can be either an internal or external examination of your business. **AUDIT** means that an external party will look at your business through a financial lens. The audit can allow you to gain objective insight into your business rather than find things you are doing wrong and penalise you for them.

Many people cringe at the thought of "the auditors coming", but auditing is one of the most helpful business tools, not just a necessary "evil". Reporting is enhanced, duplication is avoided, and accuracy throughout the organisation is improved.

Some audits are compliance-driven and statutory by nature; Health & Safety, Work Relations Committee (WRC), International Organization for Standardization (ISO), and Financial audits are primarily carried out in limited companies.

CONCLUSION

Having all relevant financial data is an absolute must if your business is to survive and thrive. There is just no way around this. Some people think an accountant, auditor or any other office-bound job is not essential to growing the business, but someone needs to maintain order and ensure that everything is running correctly to grow. We look at dashboards and Key Performance Indicators in Chapter 8.

That is why I recommend you have regular access to your accounts. They give you valuable feedback on where you are heading and allow you to adjust early before taking the next step or divert early if something negatively impacts your business. Ensure you have access to and review this information regularly and arrange a monthly meeting with relevant persons to analyse and discuss the reports.

"Life is like accounting: everything must be balanced."

Unknown

ACCOUNTS HEALTHCHECK

1. Do I have access to a Balance Sheet, a Profit and Loss Account, and Cash Flow?

2. Do I have up-to-date **ACCOUNTS PAYABLE** and **ACCOUNTS RECEIVABLE** balances to help me better understand my cash position?

3. How simple or challenging is it for me to collate and track this at any moment?

4. How can the process be simplified to track this information more efficiently?

5. How can I better use this information to improve my business?

6. Is there a **SEGREGATION OF DUTIES**? Does one person have too much control over an area, e.g. cash management?

7. Whom would I like to have on my board of **DIRECTORS**?

8. How often will I have a **BOARD MEETING**?

9. What will be discussed or on the agenda?

10. How will board decisions be communicated, actioned, measured and monitored?

NOTES

7: BUDGETS

"A budget tells your money where to go instead of wondering where it went".

Dave Ramsey, America's trusted voice on money

In this chapter, you will find answers to the following questions:

- Do you need a **BUDGET**?
- Why is it important to look ahead and **FORECAST** budgetary needs, particularly in unpredictable times?
- Why do companies allocate good **RESOURCES** to planning?
- Is there such a thing as budget updates or forecasting?
- Why is it essential for management to know their budgets inside out?
- Why is it essential to look at **VARIANCES** and actual accounts and compare them to the budget?
- What benefits and insights can you gain from historical data **ANALYSIS**?

Figure 18: *Sub-Building Blocks for Budgets*

A business budget is a spending plan or a licence to spend for your business based on your income and expenses. It identifies your available capital, estimates your spending, and helps you predict revenue. The standard approach is to create an annual **BUDGET** using historical analysis to estimate future projections.

Companies can also use **BENCHMARKING** in their budgetary processes, looking at similar industries, markets and geographic locations.

CONSIDER THESE QUESTIONS FOR YOUR BUSINESS

- ✓ Do you have access to historical budget data?
- ✓ Do you know of any similar industries that you can benchmark against?
- ✓ Do you have access to all the data required to complete an accurate budget?
- ✓ How does your business's budget compare to similar businesses?

Prioritising your budgeting is as essential as your management accounts and cash flow. Budgeting is vital for your business. You need to know your company's direction, goals and when you will achieve these targets. Much effort goes into creating accurate and meaningful business budgets, be wary of making assumptions or applying unqualified criteria to your budget. If you are estimating a percentage increase in a line item, support it with factual data that can be analysed and interrogated if necessary.

Make sure to take the time to reflect and clarify what happened in the past. What worked and what didn't work? Get your senior management team and give them accountability for their relevant areas. Your employees will feel a sense of ownership as they have created this budget, and it's up to them to manage it.

Your employees should know their department and area well enough so that creating a detailed budget will be relatively straightforward, and you can provide direction and guidance. Remember to ensure their forecast aligns with the company vision and is challenging but attainable.

If you have a budget, you can compare this to your actual results and then see if something is not working. You or the department managers can make quick and accurate decisions with the help of a budget as a guide. Not looking ahead exposes you to considerable risk, and many opportunities may be missed. If you are organised and have a plan, you can deviate from it. However, suppose you don't have a plan at all. In that case, you don't have anything to reflect on or compare against. Therefore you may continue making bad mistakes until it's noticeably detrimental to your company.

IMPROVED MOTIVATION

For many companies, the budget is increased (or decreased) by X% each year – X% increase in sales – hoping that gross margin and bottom line grow in tandem. A word of warning though - an % increase in sales can have a demotivating effect on the sales staff. When they are already working hard and doing more with less, they can feel like they are doing everything they can and that the goal is unrealistic. No business wants a demotivated salesforce! Yes, you want your business to overachieve from a financial perspective, but you must always keep in mind the impact business goals have on the people you want to deliver on those goals.

Upon budget collation, it's important to sit with each department manager and break down their sales by category and product mix. Analyse the previous few years of data by sales and margin for item, quantity and price. You can then easily see that decisions based solely on turnover may negatively affect other areas. You can put energy into sales increases *via* promotions: buy one, get one free, or three for the price of two, etc. However, while these promotions increased sales and turnover figures, they may negatively affect gross margin and work output.

There are many benefits to having a budget; it provides clarity, gives focus and helps you manage the business. You should ensure a monthly meeting to review results and get feedback from each department.

Having a clear budget in place helps everyone be on the same page. Confusion can quickly occur if everyone has a different idea of what is happening. Everyone should be able to know exactly how funds will be allocated. All department managers should be involved in their budgets, ownership and communication. This Involvement will ensure that they can spend money accordingly and communicate this to their teams.

CONSIDER THESE QUESTIONS FOR YOUR BUSINESS

- ✓ How accountable are the department managers for their budget or the variances to actual?
- ✓ Is "being on budget" a key performance indicator for your managers?
- ✓ What proactive actions do they take concerning budget management?
- ✓ How often is the budget drawn up and reviewed?
- ✓ How often are the actual figures compared to the budget?
- ✓ What variables are in the employees' control?

HISTORICAL DATA

It's imperative to have access to historical data to know what is happening in your business so you can confidently plan for the future and make accurate and informed business decisions. Historical data allows you to analyse your business year on year. Considering seasonality and other factors that may affect your business. Talk to your accountant and know how the accounts are tracked and if changes need to be made. Having this data as a starting point is essential to enable you and your team to plan a budget and look ahead.

To set up any budget, you need access to historical data and time to analyse it as much as possible – for example, sales by category, product, cost centre, department, and so on. Look at what each customer and stock item or Stock Keeping Unit (SKU) is doing for your business and consider whether you want to continue with the product or service. What market is it in, and could more markets be added? These are discussions to be had with the senior management team. Next, you can look at each item/category using the PESTLE model.

CONSIDER THESE QUESTIONS FOR YOUR BUSINESS

- ✓ Do you have access to historical data?
- ✓ Do you track sales by revenue stream?
- ✓ Do you track costs by department or category?
- ✓ Do you compare actual to budget and forecasts?
- ✓ Are you aware of seasonality and how it affects your business?

PESTLE ANALYSIS

The PESTLE model outlines all factors that may affect the budget. PESTLE stands for **P**olitical, **E**nvironmental, **S**ocial, **T**echnological, **L**egal and **E**conomic. When setting up any budget, consider all these topics concerning your business and how they may affect your sales, markets and products/services. Do you know the seasonality and all variables that affect your product or service? You can reflect this in your budget if there are changes throughout the year.

Figure 19: *PESTLE*

FORECAST

You won't have all the answers, and you don't have a magic-looking glass, so you can only predict with the information you have to hand.

The budget can be completed at the beginning of the year or before a new financial year. This budget is a guide; changes may be made as the year progresses and more realistic data comes In. This document is the forecast and forms an integral part of the company's Business Plan.

Some businesses update their business plan and budget projections throughout the year. These updates are knowns as **FORECAST**s. For example, many companies have several versions of their budget, Forecast 3+9, Forecast 5+7, Forecast 9+3 etc., meaning that they have actual data for the first few months and now predict estimates for the remaining months.

CONSIDER THESE QUESTIONS FOR YOUR BUSINESS

✓ When was the Budget completed? When is a good time to reforecast?

✓ Do you have access to financial forecasts?

✓ Could you consider conducting a PESTLE review of your Budget?

CONCLUSION

You can now see why budgets are important. They give employees direction and financial boundaries to work within and provide senior management with information on what to look out for. Your business budget will give you an accurate picture of expenditures and revenues and drive critical business decisions such as optimising marketing, and spending, hiring staff, purchasing equipment, and improving efficiencies. It also outlines your business's financial and operational goals, so you can use it as a guide to help you allocate resources, evaluate performance, and formulate action plans.

"A debt problem at its core is a budgeting problem."

Natalie Pace

BUDGET HEALTHCHECK

1. Do I have a business plan, and how do I create one if not?
2. How would my business benefit if it had a budget?
3. Who will I include in the budget process?
4. What data do I have access to for analysis?
5. How far ahead do I want budget projections?
6. What variables should I consider?
7. What are fixed versus variable costs?
8. Is my industry seasonal? What is seasonal about my industry?
9. How often will I look at the budget, and with whom?
10. How does the budget compare to the actual? Was the budget realistic?

NOTES

8: DATA ANALYSIS

"What gets measured gets managed".

Peter Drucker

In this chapter, you will find answers to the following questions:

- How and why do you need to collect and have up-to-date data to hand?
- Do you need to have live access to your data?
- What are the benefits of analysing your data, and why do you want to collect it?
- How to leverage dashboards to manage your business better?
- Why are **KEY PERFORMANCE INDICATORS (KPIs)** so important?
- What **INPUTS**, **PROCESSES** and **OUTPUTS** do you need to analyse?

Figure 20: *Sub-Building Blocks for Data Analysis*

A **DASHBOARD** contains essential data gathered within the company. It is presented graphically and can include comparisons to previous years, previous months, departments, budgets or market norms. Dashboards are an excellent investment of time because they immediately give you more control and oversight of what exactly is happening in your business. Dashboards can help optimise productivity, provide greater data visibility, and lead to better decision-making that effectively lowers your business costs. Remember, wasted time or an incorrect conclusion equals wasted money and lost opportunities.

Many companies grow fast and have employees with over 10+ years of service. Although it is fabulous to have such long-standing employees, which says a lot about the company, if employees have always worked a certain way, they may not question or challenge what is in front of them.

For that reason, you may want to task departments to question the status quo; look for new opportunities to enhance and improve processes. Remember that minor tweaks can have a significant positive impact on your business. Now, this might require a shift in mindset for some employees who are happy with how things are. A great way to kick off this activity is to review departmental strategies, key processes, customer (internal/external) feedback and budgets.

Measure departmental heads on identifying opportunities that will lower costs, increase revenue or innovate. The best way to ensure consistent collection of data for your dashboards is:

- Meet with your department heads
- Share the importance and value of the dashboards
- Provide templates and processes for them to follow this ensures consistency across all functions
- Allow shared access of calendars and important dates
- Manage closely until the teams are used to the new processes

MEETINGS

You could argue that most businesses have far too many meetings! Management meetings, team meetings, board meetings and so on. Have you recently asked yourself how productive these meetings are and if they are a good use of employees' time? A dashboard management tool can quickly and visually pinpoint problem areas in your company, detect where these problems are, and then investigate what you can do to solve them. What gets measured gets done! The dashboard Is a way of measuring data and ensuring you are keeping In line with the company and departmental objectives.

Suppose you have weekly or monthly meetings with your employees. By implementing a dashboard with critical performance measurement criteria, you will notice that the meetings will become much more productive and focused as areas of concern are quickly highlighted, targeted, and prioritised. Ensuring you are only looking at the most critical issues of the day and not wasting time on secondary issues.

Weekly meetings analysing the dashboard will identify what is happening in the company, i.e., reflecting on what is shaping the company. You can identify where improvements can be made or what actions need to be taken. Overall, you will notice improvements in the company's work rate and a significant improvement in morale, giving employees back time as less meetings are needed. When employees know the bigger picture and feel a part of it, it keeps them moving in the right direction.

DASHBOARDS

A dashboard helps promptly identify if results or outcomes are not aligned with the company's goals. It facilitates open communication based on hard facts and real data. Decisions are then made in real time as data is presented to allow informed decision-making.

If you attempt to incorporate too much data into a dashboard, it may lose its impact, so be careful not to make them too flashy or cluttered. When setting up dashboards, you must understand the dashboard constraints, users' needs, and the range of different data analysis measurements.

It's essential to ensure that all users know how to update and refresh the dashboard. You can make amendments to allow the dashboard to grow with the organisation, but the user must understand the impact of any changes on any charts within the dashboard.

Dashboards may not update automatically due to a company skills deficit, software capabilities and other constraints, and also links can drop on the dashboard. It's important to know that the information you are presenting is accurate.

Information can be downloaded to Excel or uploaded and downloaded to other systems. Many dashboard systems are available, such as Microsoft Power BI, Excel Pivot Tables, Slicers, Graphs, and Tableau. You can integrate information from most accounting software packages Into a dashboard format.

You want to ensure that the visuals you choose best represent the data you want to analyse. The visual has to tell you first-hand the answers to the questions that you may have. They can be colour-coded or specific graphs with numeric and %. Please pay close attention to how they are set up.

Implementing dashboards in your organisation is a good idea, and proper practical training can be an excellent investment. Your ability to take decisive corrective action in your business will be the real test of the value of a dashboard.

CONSIDER THESE QUESTIONS FOR YOUR BUSINESS

- ✓ How can you personalise a dashboard for your business?
- ✓ What do you want to see on your dashboard?
- ✓ What do you want to achieve from it?
- ✓ Who will be involved in setting up and monitoring the dashboard?
- ✓ How often is the dashboard updated, reviewed & by whom?

I have included examples of dashboards below. These dashboards look into four different categories:

1) Finance
2) Customers
3) Employees
4) Operations

FINANCIAL DASHBOARD

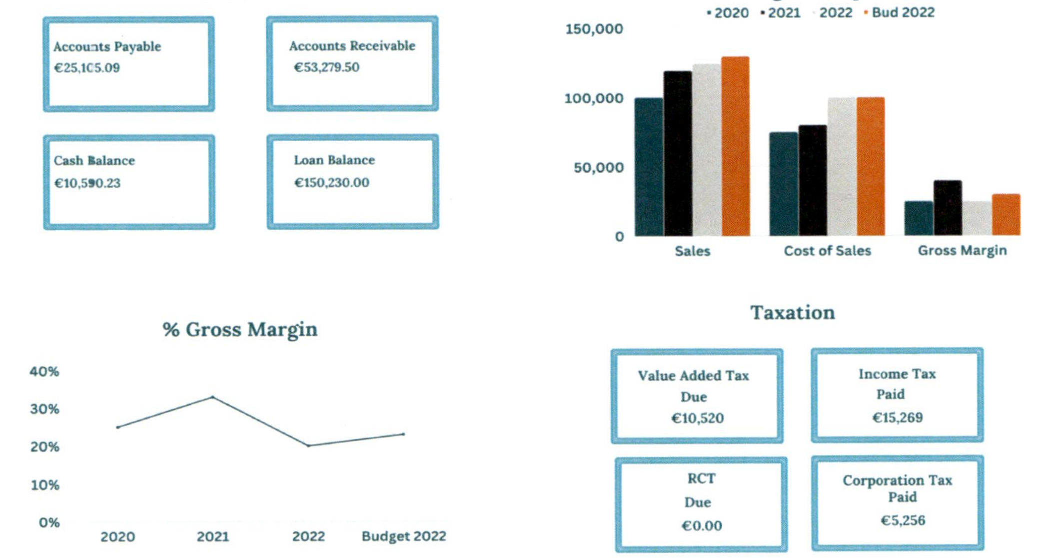

Figure 21: *Sample Financial Dashboard*

CUSTOMER DASHBOARD

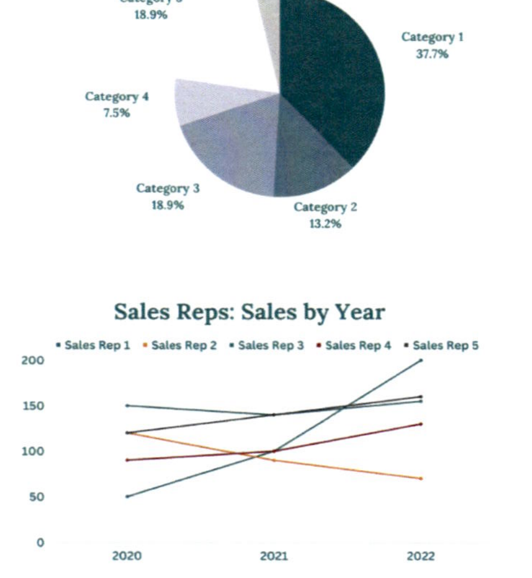

Figure 22: *Sample Customer Dashboard*

OPERATIONAL DASHBOARD

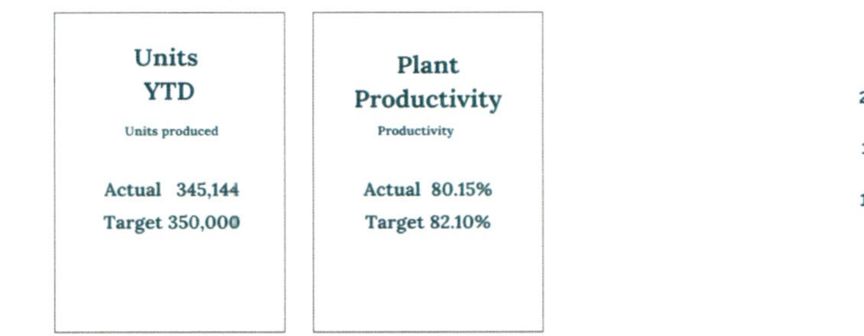

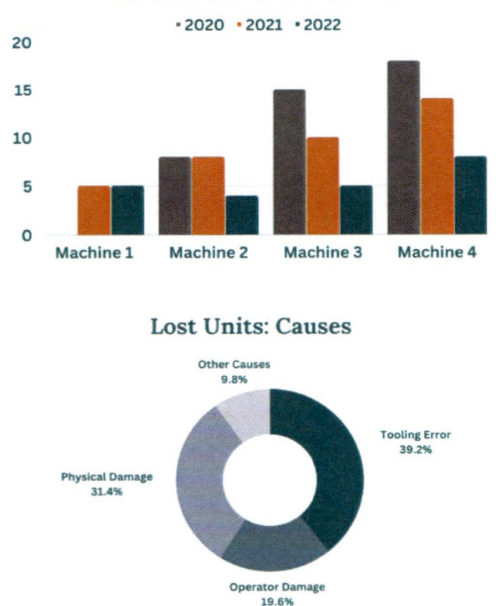

Figure 23: *Sample Operational Dashboard*

EMPLOYEE DASHBOARD

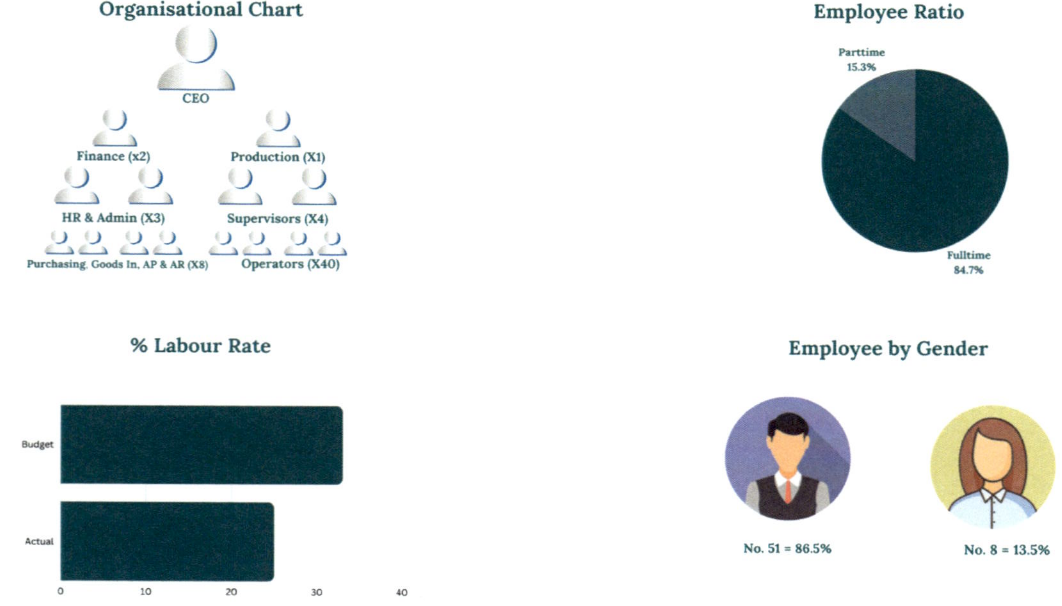

Figure 24: *Sample Employee Dashboard*

The dashboard must be easily understood so that decisions can be made quickly from them. So they have to contain all data relevant to the conclusion required. Where possible, compare them with prior-year data, with the budget, forecast or benchmarked from similar industries and taking account of seasonality.

The sooner you see a trend that is not favourable, the sooner you can make a decision and prevent the company from going further in the wrong direction and get it back on track

The more you look at a dashboard and use the most recent information, the better this is for the company. You want real-time data, as up-to-date as possible, quickly refreshed dashboards and analytical tools that automatically gather and analyse the data for you.

CONSIDER THESE QUESTIONS FOR YOUR BUSINESS

- ✓ How do you use a dashboard?
- ✓ What KPIs do you want to measure and have on the dashboard?
- ✓ Whom do you want in the meetings?
- ✓ How often do you want an updated dashboard?
- ✓ What do you want a visual representation of?
- ✓ What needs to be measured?
- ✓ Are all resources relevant to their roles available to all staff, or is more training needed?

Decide on the frequency of updates required and arrange a regular meeting to coincide with this update: weekly, monthly, quarterly, etc. When the company's goals are set out in its **VISION/MISSION**, use these goals and objectives to decide what data you will analyse and how often you want to discuss it.

The more questions you can ask, the more meaningful and relevant your dashboard will be. When you know what process occurs with each input, creating a dashboard from the tracked information and the output required is straightforward.

KEY PERFORMANCE INDICATORS

A **KPI** is a specific goal set for a task or employee aligned with the company goal. You will want to choose **KEY PERFORMANCE INDICATORS (KPIS)** for all relevant departments that align with your company goals and feed these to employees as part of their performance review process.

The clarity in KPIs is one of the many benefits of setting up and using dashboards. Be specific and clear on the overall objectives and goals of your company. Align these goals with the departments' and employees' goals and measure the output. You can then set up visuals to show you how near or far you are away from that goal. It can be presented in a chart format, by week, month, year, department etc., using any detail or layout you want.

PROCESSES

You will have numerous processes that take place in your company. i.e. the tasks carried out within your company. What inputs or triggers do you receive to start a process? The input relates to the information coming into your business, from whom and in what format. All processes lead to a final output for your company. There may be sub-processes or stages within the process, so It's important to document and streamline them as much as possible.

It's also crucial to map the processes throughout the organisation. This mapping will identify the departments involved, process steps, measurements required, inputs, outputs and formats.

Simple tools can be set up to streamline communication and information capture and processes. Who is involved at what stage, and in what format is the information collated or presented?

CONSIDER THESE QUESTIONS FOR YOUR BUSINESS

- ✓ What are your crucial business processes?
- ✓ How are they carried out?
- ✓ What input and output are expected from the process?
- ✓ Who wants this output, and in what format do they want it?
- ✓ What are the deadlines for the output?
- ✓ Do you know what people and departments are involved?
- ✓ Is the process flow mapped?
- ✓ Are processes regularly reviewed for opportunities to improve?

Some examples of KPI considerations for **INPUTS** include:

- What are the inputs into the organisation that need processing? Or kickstart the process?
- What format do they come and how often? , e.g. email, phone, website, booking system, physical location, messenger, et cetera.
- Are the inputs coming from inside the organisation or from an external source? Is this prone to change?
- Who gives these inputs to whom in the organisation? How often are there delays? How is it documented?
- Are they by e-mail, Excel, or an actual product? Can it be measured?
- What tests or processes are carried out on the input? By whom?
- What documentation is received and recorded? How often?
- How are the inputs recorded? How accurate?
- How can the input be made more efficient?
- Can the communication of the input be improved? Any complaints?
- How can you measure these?

Some examples of KPI considerations for **PROCESSES** include:

- What jobs are completed or process takes place from these inputs?
- Do we need to do this process?
- Who uses it?
- How are they assembled, and by whom?
- Are they similar to jobs carried out in other parts of the organisation?
- Is there a more efficient, effective way to get it done at less cost?
- Is there duplication of the process or part?
- Can you simplify the process?
- What checklists are in place for this process?
- Are there any templates that can be drawn to improve the process and avoid duplication?
- How are the processes measured or tracked?
- Are they time-based – for example, with so many hours or days from receipt of the input, or several inputs in a day, week, a month?
- How many times does an input have to be managed?
- How do you measure duplication or errors?

Examples of KPI considerations for **OUTPUTS** include:

- Who requires that information or product?
- Who is it going to, and what format do they need it in?
- Is it internal or external to the company?
- What is a guide timescale for this to be completed?
- When can it move to the next stage?

CONSIDER THESE QUESTIONS FOR YOUR BUSINESS

- ✓ Would it improve the workflow if you could present the information in a visual format?
- ✓ How can we measure this output?
- ✓ How often Is the information due?
- ✓ Look at critical areas of the business; what is the standard expected, and is it being met/measured?
- ✓ Are there similar processes or portions of the work completed in any other department? (Duplication?)

CONCLUSION

The aim of a meeting to discuss the company dashboard is to improve your organisation continuously and ensure that you are on track with your company objectives. The dashboard makes it easy to highlight issues quickly and helps to decide what corrective action to take.

If you can easily compare data from month to month, year to year, industry to industry, and department to department, then you can work proactively and confidently to make informed decisions.

A dashboard is not to point the finger at anyone doing something wrong, much less viewed as a performance indicator for the individual. It should be seen as a tool that can support you in finding the best possible result for any business element by learning from past mistakes and avoiding future ones. Without data analysis, it's like decision-making in the dark.

"In God we Trust. All others must bring data."

W. Edward Deming, American Engineer & Statistician

DATA ANALYSIS HEALTHCHECK

1. What dashboards do I have in my business?
2. What type of information do I want to measure?
3. Does the dashboard explain the progress towards the company's objectives?
4. How can I measure these goals at all levels within my company?
5. Are employee objectives directly aligned with the company's objective
6. How often are meetings held?
7. Who should attend the meetings?
8. What objectives are discussed?
9. Does information flow inter-departmentally? Is communication open and honest, and are all employees engaging?
10. Do all employees feel welcome to offer suggestions?

NOTES

9: TAXATION

"In this world, nothing can be more certain except death and taxes."

Benjamin Franklin

In this chapter, you will find answers to the following questions:

- Why should you have a dedicated tax accountant?
- Must you register for tax?
- Why do you need to know the difference between tax types?
- Why do you need to complete tax returns?
- Why do you pay income tax *versus* corporation tax or *vice versa*?

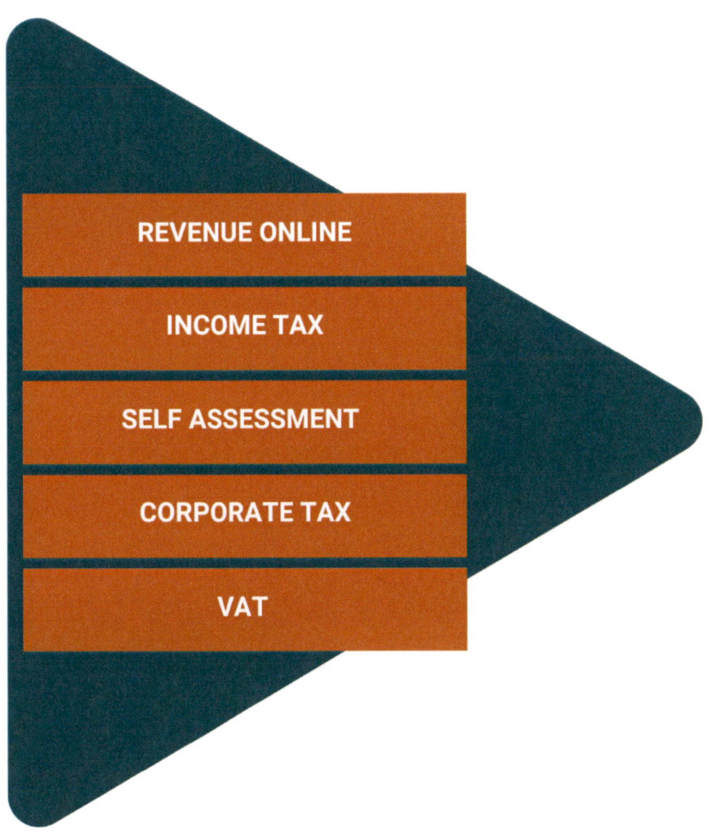

Figure 25: *Sub-Building Blocks for Taxation*

REVENUE COMPLIANCE is a must for all businesses. There are huge penalties and fines applied to companies that do not adhere to Revenue requirements and deadlines. Business owners must know their taxation requirements or have access to someone who can give them professional and reliable advice. Taxation can be complicated, and you don't know what you don't know. So if it is not an area of your expertise, find someone who can support you.

REVENUE ONLINE

When setting up any business, one of the first things you do is register your business with the **COMPANIES REGISTRATION OFFICE (CRO)** and **REVENUE**.

All companies must register their business name with the CRO. "A company registered under the Companies Act 2014 becomes a body corporate as and from the date mentioned in its certificate of incorporation. A company has a separate legal personality - it is a separate and distinct legal person. Registration of a business name does not create an entity with a different legal personality. The owner of the business name - the individual(s) or company who registered the name is the person to be contacted or sued."

CONSIDER THESE QUESTIONS FOR YOUR BUSINESS

- ✓ Are you trading as a sole trader or a limited company?
- ✓ Have you registered with the revenue department ?
- ✓ Are you obliged to charge VAT?
- ✓ Who can help you with your Corporation Tax Return?

You can easily set up with Revenue and have online access for queries and taxation returns. This online system is called the **REVENUE ONLINE SYSTEM (ROS)**. You can also give your external accountant access to ROS to ensure that all your returns are up-to-date and filed on time.

ROS is used to file both Corporation Tax, which refers to the company taxes and Income tax, related to the tax for employees. There is no escaping Revenue; you must register with Revenue to pay your taxes.

INCOME TAX

INCOME TAX is the tax you pay as an individual. If you are an employee, your company will organise this tax, **PAYE** (Pay As You Earn Tax), **PRSI** (Pay Related Social Insurance), **USC** (Universal Social Charge), and **LPT** (Local Property Tax) for you via payroll. They will deduct the tax from your gross salary, pay you the net compensation and pay the taxes due to revenue.

As a sole trader or from a business point of view, you are responsible for filing the income taxes for yourself and your employees, as mentioned above. You must ensure that all taxes are deducted and paid to Revenue within specified timelines.

If you are self-employed, you will be responsible for doing a self-assessment at the end of the financial year. A self-assessment means filing your income tax return, including paying any taxes due to Revenue within the specified timeline. Late submissions will incur charges such as penalties and interest.

SELF ASSESSMENT

SELF ASSESSMENT means that each self-employed or sole trader is responsible for completing their revenue return of taxes at the end of the calendar year. You pay **PRELIMINARY TAX** (an estimate of tax due for your current trading year) on or before 31 October each year and make a tax return for the previous year not later than 31 October.

You must understand what expenses you can claim or include in your business accounts. Know the deadline dates and contact an accountant if you cannot do this yourself. They will help you with the return's compliance element and advise on how to account for your expenses, drawings, VAT and any other questions you may have.

CORPORATION TAX

CORPORATION TAX is the tax a company pays to Revenue. Corporation tax is charged as a percentage of your profits – that is, sales, less direct costs and expenses, and any personal add-backs. Businesses typically have management accounts prepared in-house but hire an external accountant to prepare the financial statements and tax returns. Hiring an external accountant to file these returns ensures compliance, as they are familiar with Revenue requirements.

VAT

VALUE ADDED TAX is the tax on goods and services purchased and sold.

Value Added Tax

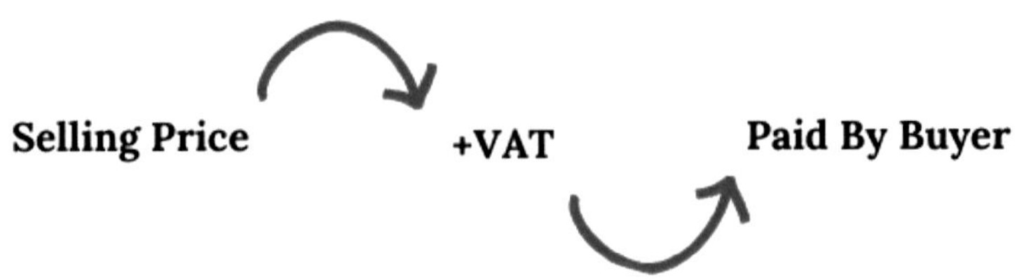

Figure 26: *Value-Added Tax*

In Ireland, if a service company's annual turnover does not exceed €37,500, you are not obliged to charge VAT on your invoices. Otherwise, all invoices for sales and purchases will have VAT on them. It's essential to know the criteria. It often changes; understand what questions to ask and find someone to help you.

You have to document all invoices and account for all VAT. You will agree on the schedule for VAT returns upon setup of the company with Revenue, usually paid every two months, but sometimes every four months, six months or annually.

The information should be easily accessible from an accounting package or wherever you collate your financial data. It's essential to adhere to the VAT return deadlines and ensure sufficient cash is set aside to pay Revenue when taxes fall due.

Documentation is a must for Revenue. All receipts and invoices must be stored and kept on file for at least six years.

There are many forms of taxation that I have not covered or mentioned in this chapter. Please get in touch with your accountant or tax advisor and know what taxes you must pay and when they fall due. Ignorance in this area is not a form of defence in court. You must comply with revenue regulations.

CONCLUSION

Organising your taxes is extremely important for the compliance and longevity of your company. I have seen great companies go through painful revenue audits because they did not have their tax documents correctly calculated. The resulting penalties can be devastating, if not lead to the company's downfall.

If all the tax payments are sorted and correctly handled, there will be much less to worry about.

"The hardest thing to understand in this world is the Income Tax."

Albert Einstein, The Theory of Relativity

TAXATION HEALTHCHECK

1. Do I know the difference between income tax and corporation tax?
2. Do I have an obligation to file a tax return?
3. How do I register for online filing - ROS?
4. What taxes should I pay and file, and by when?
5. Do I need to register for VAT?
6. What are the filing deadlines?
7. What expenses can I claim on the tax return?
8. When do I pay the income tax or corporation tax?
9. What good accountant do I know?
10. Do I need tax advice?

NOTES

10: BUSINESS SUPPORTS

"When looking for funding, don't just look for cash. Look for the right people".

Jodie Fox, Director of Fashion & Founder, Shoes of Prey

In this chapter, you will find answers to the following questions:

- Should you find out about funding and support?
- What is the best way to get funding?
- Should you apply for a grant, and what grants are available?
- What do you need to understand the tender application process?
- Why do you have to fill out grant claim forms?

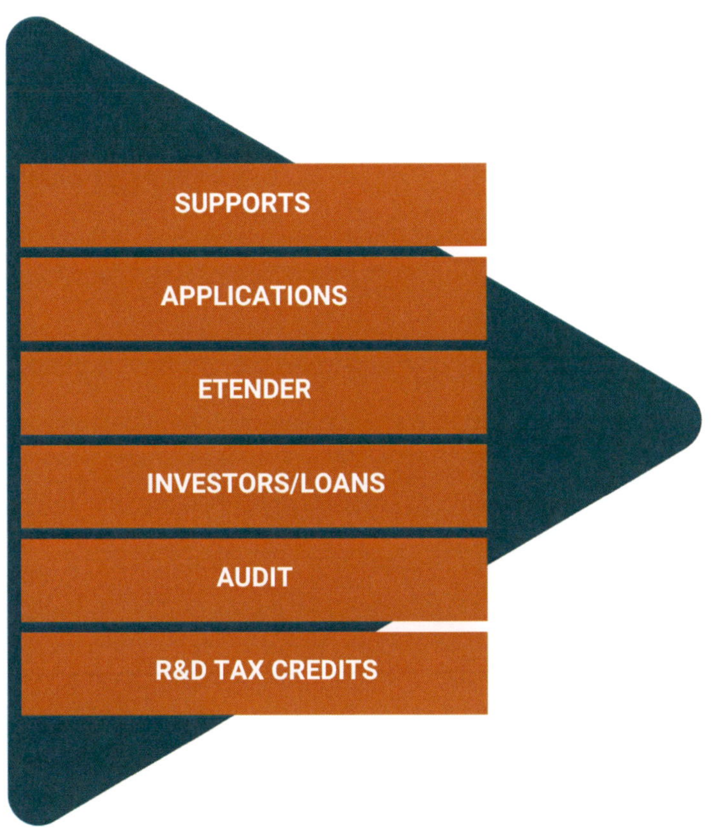

***Figure 27**: Sub-Building Blocks for Business Supports:*

SUPPORTS

Many companies have great success with funding and grant applications, and other companies never bother to apply. Some businesses can be put off by the vast document application process and don't know where to start.

- Do you know what grants and funding your business can qualify for?
- Are you familiar with other types of business support that are available?

Several funding opportunities and free consulting support are available to you and your business. The trick is to keep yourself informed and know where to look. Many agencies can help with funding. Consulting companies can work with you on the application process to ensure a successful application. They will then carry out the work after that, so it's in their interest to help you write up the application to ensure you win. Many companies apply for these tender applications all the time. They know how to write them and what to look for in the tender document. They can take the strain of the application away from you. Start by getting in contact with your local enterprise board if you are unsure who may be able to help you with tenders and applications.

APPLICATIONS

Knowing the **FUNDING APPLICATIONS** available and how to access them is essential.

Help and support come in many formats: some Cash Funding via Banks or Investors, some Financial Refunds on a Capital Expenditure that you have incurred; for example, under the Local Enterprise offices' Trading Online Voucher scheme, you pay upfront when setting up a website and get a refund later upon proof of payment to your supplier.

Others come in the form of ***VOUCHERS*** via the Local Enterprise Office or Enterprise Ireland, so it's well worth asking them what is available. Mentoring is available *via* the Small Firms Association, Skillnet Ireland, Enterprise Training Board, Intertrade Ireland, your Local Enterprise Office and many others; A mentor/consultant will work with your business but get paid separately from the relevant government agency.

There are also *grants* for training, capital expenditure, and employee recruitment via these agencies.

As a new company starting up, you may qualify for Startup Grants or High Potential Start-Up (HPSU) through Enterprise Ireland; get connected and investigate what is available to your business at its different stages.

You are not alone in business, even though it may feel that way at times; there are so many agencies set up to help. This is where networking can be a great advantage. Ask questions, keep asking questions and keep digging. If you have a problem in your business, you can be sure that someone else has been in your shoes. How did they do what they did? What funding or support were they able to access? Who did they go to for guidance and advice? For example, did you know that many agencies will pay portions of initial wages if you want to hire a new person but can't afford it?

These applications can sometimes be challenging to understand but, if successful, well worth the headache. Find a mentoring or consulting company to help you write the tender application. Because no matter what level of investment you are looking for, there are ways to get cash access from €2,000 to €2,000,000. Don't let cash be a problem if you fully believe in your product or service. Ask questions and find out who can help. Good recordkeeping and reporting will be essential when applying for these grants and loans.

Banks can charge high-interest rates, so if there are alternative solutions to access cash, it is worth your while knowing them, right?

CONSIDER THESE QUESTIONS FOR YOUR BUSINESS

- ✓ What agencies are you linked with or could you connect to, and what other agencies could you contact to ask about mentoring or funding?
- ✓ What are the sources of mentoring or funding available for your business?
- ✓ Are you hiring more staff or investing heavily in capital equipment?
- ✓ Have you received funding in the past or got refunded for mentoring undertaken?
- ✓ Have you registered with etenders? i.e.? Are you actively using it?
- ✓ Can you identify an employee who is good with applications and may help in this area?
- ✓ Do you know any other business owners you can ask about these vouchers or supports?

ETENDER

ETENDERS.ie is a government site for public tenders, where all public tenders are advertised. It is simply an online portal to register, apply for tenders, and complete your tendering process. e.g. etenders. You should be aware that you can apply for tenders as a company. If you qualify, you can get financial help from the government, opening up new pathways for your business.

It is worth getting set up on etenders and attending etender courses to allow you to note the critical points, practices and feedback for successful applications. These courses will let you know what to look out for or avoid. Many local training companies will have a day course on the etender application process.

Some fundamental criteria for all tender applications are set out in the **REQUEST FOR TENDER (RFT)**. Reading the RFT document and familiarising yourself with the requirements, dates, timelines, etc., relevant to the tender application is necessary. Crossing the T's and dotting the I's is essential, or your application may be considered invalid, ignored or delayed.

You are also allowed to ask questions, follow these and get answers to questions others have asked. Ensure that you read these, know any updates, and have the latest application form for submission.

There are no exceptions to late submissions. Know the cut-off times and have all information ready for upload as early as possible. There are also criteria around the size and format of documents, so ensure that you have these submitted in the correct format.

When successful on a tender, it's a great way to be introduced to new customers; you can provide your services and work with them via the application you have won at no cost to the customer. Therefore they will get to know your services and may continue to work with you after the program is complete.

STEPS INVOLVED IN ETENDER APPLICATION
✓ Request for Tender created and uploaded to an online portal
✓ Suppliers invited to apply
✓ Responses received and submitted within the timeframe
✓ Responses analysed
✓ Contract awarded to the more eligible supplier
✓ The eligible supplier manages the contract

INVESTORS / LOANS

There are many ways to raise capital. Asking a **Family or Friend** for Capital may be the best solution. They might be happy to lend you cash for the short term, share your business interest, or become partners.

Mixing business and pleasure is not always easy, and many good relationships have been hurt by not having the proper communication and expectations. Don't lend money lightly to family or friends. Ensure that you take this process professionally.

You can also apply to your local bank for a **BUSINESS LOAN**. It helps if you have a good business plan to convince banks to lend to you.

You might also want to consider private investors, who are split into two main types "Angel Investors" and "Venture Capitalists". Both investors will typically receive shares in the company in return for their investment, but these shares are not publicly traded.

An **ANGEL INVESTOR** is a high net-worth individual with access to money, resources and the background to make a company successful. They usually come in at the early stages of a business. An Angel Investor is likely to contribute enough money so that no other investors are needed. However, angel investors expect a high investment return, and the business case has to be airtight. They will be part of the day-to-day operations of the company. They will have a voice in the development of the business. Online sites or network groups are some ways to find/connect with Angel Investors.

When a business is expanding and heading into a riskier venture, **VENTURE CAPITALISTS** are needed. Venture capitalists use investors' money, not their own; They do this by setting up a fund for others to buy shares in the relevant company.

Venture Capitalists can help startups, but they usually come into established businesses with solid management teams that have already been proven successful. That business is now diversifying or growing and needs money.

Venture capitalists usually invest more than Angel Investors, which can be in the millions. The prediction is that the return on investment will also be very high. Venture capitalists will also own shares in the company and have a say in the business's day-to-day running.

There are many other ways to get investors and access to cash. So look around, ask questions, join network groups similar to your industry and don't be afraid to have confidence in your business and the product/service you provide.

AUDIT

Regarding the funding or tendering process, having access to proper records demonstrates your business's compliance with the relevant governing body. If audited by the client tendering the work or the organisation offering the funding, you need access to all the documents they may ask for, for example, banking records, payments, invoices, payslips and other business reports or contracts.

Know your audit requirements and be compliant with all relevant regulatory bodies. If you don't have the right skillset in-house, consider hiring or outsourcing the skill to acquire the knowledge of what you should keep, for how long, and be audit ready. Maintaining the correct information as you go along is so much easier than collating when required.

R&D TAX CREDITS

Some companies carry out **RESEARCH AND DEVELOPMENT (R&D)** unknown to themselves. They are so skilled in engineering, and what comes naturally to them, don't realise this activity falls into the category of R&D. Could this be you?

If it is, you may be able to apply for R&D Tax Credits via Revenue. Any auditing firms will discuss this with you and show you what you can apply for. You may also be able to backdate it to the previous year.

All details are in the Revenue document, as seen in the link below. It is very detailed, and as such, it's cumbersome and puts people off applying, but the rewards are well worth the effort.

https://www.revenue.ie/en/companies-and-charities/reliefs-and-exemptions/research-and-development-rd-tax-credit/index.aspx

Details around R&D Revenue application and what to look out for, for now, to help in future:

- Saving all documentation;
- Minutes of all meetings;
- Document jobs by number – can keep R&D separate numbering system if more accessible;
- Photos at different stages; or scribbles of drawings and prototypes;
- Where do you save things? E-mails? System? Use job numbers on all communications.
- Sub-contract work can be used in R&D applications. Max of €100k or 15% of Subcontractors' cost;

- Collaborations with colleges and universities can be discussed, and % included also;
- If grants are already applied for through other agencies, deduct these grants from the final claim.

Consider a time management system and have a backup for documentation of hours used in preparation for the application. Are all jobs coded, and are employees putting their hours into the correct jobs? Ensure that the dates are recorded correctly, i.e., holidays do not overlap with hours used in the application. The information must be valid, accurate and correct.

Set up job cards for employees or templates to document the jobs they are working on. Templates to write information on the job. Allocate an employee to write up minutes of meetings to track the progress.

Was a prototype sent from your company? How long can people work on it by phone call, zoom meetings etc.? This time can be used in an application.

Someone will look at the bio of all employees included in the application; this can be done in advance. What qualifications do the critical personnel have? How many years of experience? Write up each bio using a consistent template; you can look through CVs and Human Resource files subject to privacy but get feedback from the employee. Further qualifications may not have been given to the employer in recent years.

Know what costs are eligible. Set up templates to track this or pass it on to another person to maintain each year. Consider what to include and what to exclude. What are the milestones for this project? Where is the R&D job within the milestones? A technical expert must write up a detailed application, unlike a financial expert who will put the financial data together.

R&D - THINGS TO CONSIDER

✓ Activities classified as Qualifying R&D

✓ Project descriptions

✓ Importance of dates

✓ What are the scientific tests?

✓ Costs allocation, what costs apply?

✓ Who are and what information do you need for Key Personnel?

✓ Working with 3rd party Contractors

✓ Linking with 3rd-level institutions

✓ R&D within Group Companies

✓ How to treat grants received

✓ Calculating the Tax credit

✓ Limit the number of payable credits & carry forward tax credits

✓ Analysis of the final R&D application to Revenue

CONCLUSION

Government funding and supports are available to companies. You don't have to go it alone; you can build a great company through hard work and dedication, but why not accept a helping hand along the way?

If you have the opportunity to apply and accept funding, go for it. I advise that the best time to look for funding is when you don't want it. That is when you can use the funds for growing your business instead of putting out possible fires.

The discipline in this book and the collation of management accounts, forecasts and cash flow will help you with potential future investors should you wish to go down that route.

"Investing is laying out money now to get more money back in the future."

Warren Buffet, American Business Investor and Philanthropist

FUNDING HEALTHCHECK

1. Am I entitled to funding?

2. Who can help me know my funding eligibility?

3. Who can help me with the application?

4. R&D Tax Credits - What is it? Where can you get more information?

5. Am I a member of a Local Enterprise Office?

6. What are the critical criteria for grant claims?

7. Is all critical documentation readily available if requested?

8. If not, who within my company is good with documentation?

9. Is there any value in talking to Angel Investors or Venture capitalists?

10. Whom can I talk to who has been through these processes before?

NOTES

FINAL WORDS

I hope you can see and have learned the importance of building solid business foundations; it is the cornerstone of a thriving business.

Remember to keep focused on getting these basics right.

Make sure to give yourself time to internalise all information contained in this book. It will enable you to see your business from a different perspective. This perspective gives you distance, choice, awareness and the knowledge to fully control your business. You have the potential to improve your business further with this information and your new mindset.

You can repeatedly go back to each chapter, and even though you ask the same questions, you will be surprised to see how different your answers can be over time.

I trust that you have enjoyed this book and journey with me and will continue to rise to another level in your business. Remember that I am here for you if and when you need guidance.

https://www.maryhayden.com/

ABBREVIATIONS

ABC	ALWAYS BE CLOSING
BI	BUSINESS INTELLIGENCE
CT	CORPORATION TAX
EBIT	EARNINGS BEFORE INTEREST AND TAX
EI / EQ	EMOTIONAL INTELLIGENCE, also known as EMOTIONAL QUOTIENT
ERP	ENTERPRISE RESOURCE PLANNING.
GDPR	GENERAL DATA PROTECTION REGULATION
H&S	HEALTH AND SAFETY
HPSU	HIGH POTENTIAL STARTUP
ISO	INTERNATIONAL ORGANISATION FOR STANDARDS
IT	INCOME TAX
IT	INFORMATION TECHNOLOGY
KPI	KEY PERFORMANCE INDICATOR
LPT	LOCAL PROPERTY TAX
MIS	MANAGEMENT INFORMATION SYSTEM
NLP	NEUROLINGUISTIC PROGRAMMING
P&L	PROFIT AND LOSS
PAYE	PAY AS YOU EARN
PDR	PERSONAL DEVELOPMENT REVIEW
PRSI	PAY-RELATED SOCIAL INSURANCE
R&D	RESEARCH AND DEVELOPMENT
R&M	REPAIR AND MAINTENANCE
RFT	REQUEST FOR TENDER
ROS	REVENUE ONLINE SYSTEM
SEO	SEARCH ENGINE OPTIMISATION

TNA	**TRAINING NEEDS ANALYSIS**
USC	**UNIVERSAL SOCIAL CHARGE**
VAT	**VALUE ADDED TAX**

TERMINOLOGY

ACCOUNTING PACKAGE: a system used to manage the financial activities of a company.

ACCOUNTS PAYABLE: outstanding supplier invoices for goods or services they delivered. These invoices are yet to be paid.

ACCOUNTS RECEIVABLE: the amount of money to receive from customers for goods or services you delivered.

ANGEL INVESTOR: a high net worth individual with access to money, resources and the background to make a company successful.

AUTOMATION: refers to the process of reducing human intervention in repetitive tasks.

BALANCE SHEET: the net of all assets and liabilities in your business – for example, if you sold everything in the morning, what your business is worth on paper.

BENCHMARKING: looking at similar industries and seeing where they are at. How do you compare? Do you know of any similar industries that you can benchmark from?

BUDGET: using historical analysis and many other market indicators, industry norms and assumptions to create future projection.s

BUSINESS INTEGRATION: refers to the strategy to integrate, automate and optimise all business elements.

BUSINESS OWNER: an individual or entity who owns a business to profit from the company's successful operations.

BUSINESS PLAN: a written document to describe your business, your company objectives, your company strategies, the market you will operate in and your financial forecasts.

CAPITAL EXPENDITURE: a term used when buying a physical asset for use in the business and not to be sold within the near future.

CAPITAL: money invested in the company.

CASH INFLOW: money coming into the business relating to customer payments, debtor receipts, proceeds from the disposals of assets, investor funds or bank loan receipts.

CASH OUTFLOW: money going out of the business relating to staff wages, overhead payments, purchase of new assets, bank loan repayments, or taxation payments.

CASHFLOW STATEMENT: list of opening bank balance, plus potential amounts due in and out owing, to give an estimate of closing bank balance at a point In time.

CASHFLOW: the cash and cash equivalents being transferred into and out of business.

CORPORATION TAX (CT): the tax that a company pays on its profits at the end of the financial year.

CREDITORS: also referred to as Trade Creditors, an accounting term relating to an individual or company that has invoiced your company for goods delivered or services provided and are still outstanding.

CULTURE: in an organisation relates to "How we do things around here?" or "How things are done around here when the manager is absent or if you don't give clear instructions?". Culture also refers to the country where people were born, the ideas, customs, and social behaviour of a particular people or society.

CURRENT ASSETS: refers to assets that can be sold quickly or converted to cash easily and used in standard business operations – for example, the balance of stock, debtors (how much the customer has not yet paid) or bank balance.

DASHBOARD: contains essential data gathered within the company presented graphically, compared to previous years, previous months, departments, budgets or market norms.

DATA ANALYSIS: a term used to identify and discuss information based on information collected and usually displayed in a dashboard format or downloaded from a system.

DATA INPUTS: What type of information is coming to you? Who is it coming from, and in what format does it arrive? For example, telephone, email, letter, fax, word of mouth.

DE MINIMIS AID: a term put on the allocation of state aid – for example, grant or equity.

DEBTORS: a list of outstanding customer invoices for which the business has not yet received payment.

DIRECTORS: a board of people who manage or oversee the business.

EARNINGS BEFORE INTEREST & TAX (EBIT): the profit before any Interest or tax Is accounted for.

EMOTIONAL INTELLIGENCE / EMOTIONAL QUOTIENT (EQ): refers to the ability to identify and manage one's own emotions, as well as the emotions of others.

ENTERPRISE RESOURCE PLANNING (ERP): the consolidated process of gathering and organising business data through an integrated software package, covering sales, production, accounts and more.

ENTREPRENEUR: a person who manages and operates a business or businesses, taking on greater than normal financial risks to do so.

ETENDER: a government site that puts up all public tenders that you can apply for online – that is, make a formal offer or a bid to secure a contract.

EXTERNAL CUSTOMER: refers to any customers that buy your product.

FIXED ASSETS: refers to the physical material things you have purchased for use in your company – for example, a building, a vehicle, a computer, office equipment

FORECAST: a prediction of what you want to happen in your business.

FREE CASH FLOW: relates to the net effect of all cash inflows and outflows.

FUNDING APPLICATION: a form that a business must be fully complete before being awarded funding, and must include all information requested in the document to be a valid application.

FUNDING: refers to government or organisation money allocated to business and usually provided for a particular use. Support can include money refunded for consultancy or help to carry out a specific project.

GENERAL DATA PROTECTION REGULATION (GDPR): a set of strict privacy and security laws for companies on collecting and targeting information on people.

GROSS MARGIN: relates to the total sales less the cost of goods or services to carry out that sale.

INCOME TAX: personal taxes, which employees or sole traders regularly pay to Revenue.

INPUT: the resources required to accomplish a task – for example, time, money or effort.

INTERNAL CUSTOMER: refers to your employees and managers.

KEY PERFORMANCE INDICATOR (KPI): what is the crucial information you want to measure? And then how will you present it in the dashboard?

LEAN: ultimately means continuous improvement with customer value in mind. All employees have a role in knowing they can impact by adding value and improving their specific area.

LIABILITIES: a list of what you owe from your company – for example, bank loans, supplier invoices, taxes and wages due for payment.

LOCAL COMMUNITIES: any organisation, public or private, set up to help businesses through mentoring, training or sharing of contacts.

LONG TERM LIABILITIES: refers to money owed that is not due to be paid within one year – for example, long-term loans to the bank or an investor.

MANAGEMENT ACCOUNTS: consist of a Profit and Loss Account, a Cashflow statement, and a Balance Sheet.

MANAGEMENT INFORMATION SYSTEM (MIS): refers to any system in an organisation for the collection of data or information.

MANDATORY TRAINING: an organisation may deem specific training essential for employees to carry out a particular role or task. It also may be legally required and compulsory to enable an employee to complete their job safely and efficiently.

MARGIN: the net of revenue and direct material and labour (the direct costs your business has that are specific to the sale).

MISSON: why your business exists, and what are the goals or objectives you have outlined for it.

NETWORKING: the process of interacting with other like-minded people or with people with whom you share a common interest, almost always to develop a professional and mutually beneficial relationship.

OBJECTIVE: refers to the goals of the business – for example, Profitability, Growth, Stability, Efficiency and Survival.

OPERATING PROFIT: the net amount of sales, direct costs and overheads.

OPERATIONS: refers to the work of managing your business's inner workings to ensure that everything runs as efficiently as possible.

OUTPUTS: what output do you want to achieve from the process? Who requires this, and in what format do they want it?

OVERDRAFT: refers to a facility with your bank so that if you don't have enough cash and you want to pay a bill, the amount will still go out of your account and allow your bank balance to go into a negative.

OVERHEADS: refers to all business expenses, insurance, rent, wages, light and heat and many more.

PERSONAL DEVELOPMENT REVIEW (PDR): refers to a yearly review between the Manager and Employee. A PDR is to motivate the employee and ensure they benefit from their hard work and commitment to the company.

PRELIMINARY TAX: an estimate of tax due for your current trading year.

PROCESS: relates to the task undertaken. When an employee receives an instruction or an input, what steps are involved in getting the required output?

PROFIT & LOSS: an income statement that shows a company's performance, how much money you earn from customers *versus* how much you had to spend. The difference is net profit

REPAIR & MAINTENANCE (R&M): the cost for the upkeep of building or machinery.

REQUEST FOR TENDER (RFT): a document with an application or tender. It contains all the rules and specifics of the application.

RESEARCH & DEVELOPMENT (R&D): refers to the carrying out of innovative activity for the organisation in the field of science or technology. The primary goal is an introduction of a new product or qualitative improvement to a current product.

RESEARCH AND DEVELOPMENT (R&D) TAX CREDITS: tax credit entitlement which nets against future Corporation Tax or cash refund to companies for carrying out R&D activities.

REVENUE ONLINE SYSTEM (ROS): an online tax system used for Income Tax and Corporation Tax. You set up an account and complete your tax returns online. For example, in Ireland, revenue.ie / ros.ie.

SHAREHOLDERS: anyone that has invested in the business and holds a portion of the share capital.

SOCIAL MEDIA: websites and mobile apps that enable users to share content or to participate in networks

STAKEHOLDERS: investors and any person with interest in the business – for example, banks, suppliers, insurance, investors, directors.

STATUTORY TRAINING: a statutory body can dictate what an organisation must provide based on specific legislation.

STRATEGY: the plan of action required to achieve a long-term goal, like a well-defined road map, a crucial part of which Is understanding competitive advantage.

STREAMLINE: make a process or organisation as efficient as possible.

SUPPLY CHAIN MANAGEMENT: the flow of goods and services to and within a company. It starts with buying and storing raw materials and processing those materials until the finished goods are sold to the customer.

VALUE ADDED TAX (VAT): a tax on Goods and Services.

VALUES: refers to your belief system or set of traits in running your business – for example, honesty, quality, fun, boldness.

VARIANCES: the differences between two figures – for example, budget compared to what happened or prior year compared to what happened this year.

VENTURE CAPITALISTS: financing when a business is expanding and heading into a riskier venture. Venture capitalists use investors' money, not their own. They do this by setting up a fund for others to buy shares in the relevant company.

VISION: the ideal end state, the direction you see your business going.

WASTE: refers to unused or damaged materials and to all inefficiencies in processes and business practices.

WELL-BEING: the company will look at well-being from an employee's point of view and ensure they are comfortable in their environment. When the employee is happy and healthy, and in a good state of mind, they will do the job well and more than the job description asks of them.

WORKING CAPITAL: the net cash of current assets and current liabilities. It's essential to have a positive working capital to know that you have more money coming in than is going out.